Mike R
Aug. 23

M000233678

done

TERRY M. BOARDMAN, born in Wales in 1952, graduated with a BA History (Hons) from Manchester University. He lived and worked in Japan for 10 years and currently resides in the West Midlands, England, where he works as a freelance lecturer, writer and translator of German and Japanese. He is also the author of *Kaspar Hauser — Where did he come from?* (2006). His website is: www.threeman.org

'The Kaiser's Dream' from The Truth, 26 December 1890

MAPPING THE MILLENNIUM

Behind the Plans of
the New World Order

Terry M. Boardman

TEMPLE LODGE

Temple Lodge Publishing
Hillside House, The Square
Forest Row, RH18 5ES

www.templelodge.com

Published by Temple Lodge 1998
Reprinted 2013

© Terry M. Boardman 1998

The moral right of the author have been asserted under the Copyright, Designs and Patents Act, 1988

All rights reserved. No part of this publication may be reproduced, stored in a retrieval system, or transmitted, in any form or by any means, electronic, mechanical, photocopying, recording or otherwise, without the prior permission of the publishers

A catalogue record for this book is available from the British Library

ISBN 978 1 906999 48 3

Cover by Morgan Creative, showing detail from 'The Kaiser's Dream', *The Truth*, 26 December 1890

Typeset by DP Photosetting, Aylesbury, Bucks
Printed and bound in Great Britain by Berforts Ltd., Herts.

Contents

Introduction

While the present book may be said to have its roots in the past — the desire of a teenager in the 1960s to understand the Great War of 1914-18 — it is not a study of that conflict. Its main concern is with the present and the future: how are we, as a world community, to understand where we are and where we are going? Amidst all the hyperbole about 'the end of the millennium' and 'the dawn of the twenty-first century' there seems precious little real understanding of what the twentieth century was all about. This was evident in 1989-91 when the Soviet Union and its puppet states vanished, bringing the twentieth century effectively to an end. In the 1990s we could be said to have been in a state of limbo between two eras. So many times in 1989-91 one heard or saw written: 'Who would have believed it just a few years ago? Who could have foreseen it?' And yet so much intelligence, so much money, will-power and human feeling had gone into sustaining the Cold War, which had first appeared during the First World War. When Napoleon abolished the Holy Roman Empire in 1806 he abolished a ghost; few paid much attention to the passing of an institution that had died centuries before. But the Soviet Union had been a very real, even vigorous presence for millions throughout most of the twentieth century. So many in the West had for 40 years believed it capable of destroying the entire world.

This book began out of a desire, some 30 years ago, to understand why Europe had plunged into the abyss of the Great War, perceived by so many, then as now, as a catastrophe which would lead inexorably to the other catastrophes of the twentieth century. As this abnormally tumultuous century draws to a close, it is clear to many that a significant number of the issues, problems and challenges that faced the world before the First World War—the cataclysmic event that could with justification be said to have marked the real birth of the century—remain fundamentally unsolved at its end. Such problems include those relating to nationalism, technology, and the nature of art and its effects on society, for example. This book will not attempt to discuss the many radical social, scientific and artistic changes that were ushered in by the Great War of 1914–18, but it is widely recognized that in the historical inkling of those four short years 'we were all changed'; society would never be the same again. The solid comfortable positivism of the Victorian and Edwardian eras vanished like a chimera. By 1914 it had in any case been but the external uniform of society masking a maelstrom of seething anxieties and antipathies. The War suddenly released titanic inhuman forces which seemed to erupt from within modern humanity's collective breast; so many felt themselves to be the passive instruments or playthings of forces whose will they could in no way resist.

Conventional academic explanations of the causes of the First World War seemed very unsatisfactory to me, a teenager in the 1960s; many official diplomatic documents were still unreleased and unavailable to scrutiny due to official secrecy laws. This did not prevent historians from making one-sided claims about who was mainly 'responsible' for the War. Although more archive material has come to light since then, and a rather more balanced picture is now possible, I feel that prevailing views of the War remain unconvincing.

Such views can broadly be summarized in two categories, much beloved of media pundits: the cock-up theory and the conspiracy theory. The former maintain that European civilization as a whole was somehow responsible, owing to its fundamental contradictions. The War, they claim, was somehow inevitable; European civilization had become a time bomb waiting to go off; no individual or group, no one

nation or class can be held 'responsible'. The cock-up
theorists like to imagine that they deal with more complex,
more adult problems, and that therefore they deserve to be
taken more seriously, while the conspiracy theorists, they
say, are more simplistic, even jejune, invariably seeking for
crass or single explanations for fearsomely convoluted
problems. The modern intellectual likes to think that he is
complex, deep, ambiguous. The conspiracy theorists – a
very broad group – seek the causes of the event either in the
deliberate actions and more or less conscious attitudes of
particular individuals (the Kaiser sought by means of
imperial and military expansion to compensate for the
inferiority complex he had due to his withered arm, etc), or
else of particular groups: the war was caused by the
abnormalities of German development: German society had
been 'warped' by mysticism, Romanticism, and Prussian
militarism since Napoleonic times, so its leaders demanded
their place in the sun; the British, cynically self-interested
and morbidly anxious about a perceived loss of 'national
vitality', were determined to prevent anyone from taking
over their dominant imperial role; the French were prepared to risk world conflagration for the sake of their selfish
obsession with Alsace-Lorraine, and so forth. Each one of
these single impulses is taken by different conspiracy theorists to be *the* prime cause of the catastrophe, even if not
the only one.

The European Union movement since the Second World
War has grown not least out of a desire to try to avoid
repetition of what has been called the European Civil War
of 1914–45, and reflecting the more harmonious and less
stridently nationalistic mood of the times, there is now
among academics an inclination to refrain from casting
aspersions and blame on any particular national group.
This has led to the current domination of the cock-up theory
of the causes of the First World War: nobody was really at
fault. This makes all good Europeans feel better, but it is not

necessarily the truth. Indeed, it seems obvious to this writer that the 'truth' lies in a combination of cock-up and conspiracy. A humorous image might illustrate the problem. A young man is walking along the road day-dreaming and looking at the sky without noticing where he is going. A family relative, a jaded jealous uncle, for instance, who hates his nephew and wishes him ill, decides to hide in the bushes and throw a banana skin in his nephew's path, so that he will fall and injure himself. The nephew then does fall and nearly breaks his back. Who is the more responsible for the victim's injury, the one with the consciously malicious intention or the one who failed to pay attention to what he should have been doing? Surely both can be said to be 'responsible'. A comprehensive study of the event would seek to examine the reasons behind the jealous relative's action and the reasons for the young man's absent-mindedness. From this point of view, this book can be said to align itself more with the conspiracy theorists, but it does so out of a desire to balance prevailing trends; it does not wish to insist that all the answers are here.

To plot a course through the twenty first century that will correspond to the proper needs of human development and of this planet which sustains us, we need to know where we are in the ocean of time and through which waters we have just sailed. Otherwise, like Columbus, we are likely to end up in a place we did not intend because we were heading in entirely the wrong direction. We therefore need to have accurate knowledge of the nature of the winds that were blowing us across the sea of the twentieth century in order to decide whether we wish to continue to be blown by them through the twenty-first century or not.

Since the assassination of President Kennedy in 1963 and especially in the 1990s, numerous groups of conspiracy theorists have emerged, notably in the USA, who seek to put forward their own explanations of modern history (in some cases their conspiracies reach back millennia!) and their views of humanity's destiny in the twenty-first century and beyond. That mushroom phenomenon of the 90s, the Internet, is already teeming with such ideas, which range from the sober and well-reasoned to the utterly bizarre and paranoid. The UFO cult which has grown up since the Second World War to reach near alternative religion status for millions in these days of pre-millenarian tension has contributed much to spread suspicion of government, élites, and bureaucracies. The hippy generation of the 1960s, who opened themselves up to the most weird and wonderful (and sometimes nonsensical) notions in their efforts to liberate themselves from conventional constraints, have 'matured' in the 1980s and 1990s, and this has also had its effect on the growth of conspiracy theory. The hippies, often either as a result of drugs or some kind of spiritual experience, came to recognize the existence of other realities than the visible physical one. Such experiences naturally predisposed them at least to entertain 'occult' notions and explanations. The word 'occult' after all means 'hidden'. It was but a short step from this to the feeling that 'hidden forces' were at work in politics and society. This was a notion familiar in East Asia, for example, where belief in invisible realities has remained stronger and more tenacious than in the more materialistic West. Since the days of their cloistered ex-emperors a thousand years ago, who wielded real power from the safety of monasteries while their sons 'ruled', the Japanese, for example, have long known that those with real political power often choose to veil themselves.

The welter of conspiracy theories of the occult or non-occult variety can be utterly confusing for one who ventures into such realms. Umberto Eco satirized them very effectively in his novel *Foucault's Pendulum* to the point where any educated person reading that novel would come to the conclusion 'Well, I certainly don't want to waste my time with any of that nonsense!' But such a conclusion would shut the reader's mind to the definite streams of esoteric knowledge that have run through western society for centuries and which have immeasurably fertilized western civilization. There is in fact a considerable amount of genuine intuition, like jewels in a rubbish pile, among the conspiracy theories of our time. The problem is how to distinguish those gems from the garbage. Many of the theories, especially the techno-occult ones, remain enmeshed in the most crass kind of materialism. One needs an overview, to distinguish the wood from the trees. I found the most helpful, convincing and sober overview in the work of Rudolf Steiner, the one esotericist left out of Eco's literary assault on western esotericism.

Steiner's insights into the Great War and twentieth-century history

The twentieth century could indeed be said to have begun with the Great War, in which were rooted many of the main features that have marked the century (Russian Communism and Fascism, to name but two). In seeking to investigate what really lay behind the outbreak of the catastrophe in 1914, and thus to grasp something of the nature of the twentieth century that developed out of the War, I was greatly helped by indications and statements made during and after the War by the Austrian philosopher and spiritual scientist Rudolf Steiner (1861–1925), statements which seemed to issue from a profundity and clarity of insight that far surpassed the thoughts of the academic researchers I had encountered. This was because Steiner's ideas about the War were rooted in research of a far wider and more comprehensive scope than the very narrow purlieus of the academicians. Steiner's life-work, which he called spiritual science or anthroposophy ('wisdom of man'), was an attempt to expand the scientific mode of consciousness beyond the narrow limits of the five senses in a thoroughly clear and non-mystical way. Modern civilization, he

Rudolf Steiner, 1915

claimed, would never solve its most pressing problems as long as it restricted itself to a materialistic investigation of the merely sense-perceptible world (in which he included the worlds perceptible through the telescope, the microscope and other scientific instruments).

At the centre of Steiner's thought about history was a view of the evolution not merely of the human body, as with Darwin, but more particularly of human *consciousness*. This described the development from the childlike (not childish) stage of a dreamier mythic consciousness that was more aware of a spiritual world than a physical one, down into a grasping of physical reality to the point where modern humanity had come to regard the spiritual plane with the same disdain and disbelief with which its ancestors had regarded the physical. For the ancient Indians, the physical world was maya, illusion. Nor was this consciousness confined to the East. The medieval Christian Church burned heretics because it considered their immortal souls more important than their bodies. For many people in the late nineteenth and twentieth centuries, by contrast, the spiritual world has become illusion, and only the physical is real.

In his many lectures and books Steiner showed how this process from a spiritually centred to a materially centred world-view was unavoidable if the freedom of the human individuality were to develop. Man had to leave his spiritual home and his spiritual parents, the Gods of old, even turn his back on them, in order to win through to control over his own life. The Gods, like truly loving parents, had to withdraw and leave man in a state of increasing spiritual darkness. In that darkness man naturally came in time to doubt the very existence of a spiritual world, but in it he was able to awaken to himself and realize that he is ultimately responsible for his life. But the process is by no means completed; the evolution of consciousness continues.[1] The darkness of doubt and alienation must not be allowed to congeal into a solid rock of fear and hate that threatens the existence of humanity itself. Materialism — the obsession with the physical, which produces 'isms' such as racism, nationalism, sexism, ageism and other kinds of attachment to physical forms — must be transcended if it is not to lead to the utter destruction of civilization. The future of humanity need not be one which is dominated simply by a more ingenious mineral or biochemical technology, one which makes us all into cybernauts or cyborgs; equally it need not be one which reduces us to animality, our bodies filled with spare parts from other species and our minds driven mainly by animalistic desires for food, sex, and domination, our highest philosophy an imitation of the animal principle of the survival of the fittest.

Steiner pointed with great clarity to the *spiritual* origins of thinking and of ideas, including the idea of materialism itself. For one such as he who was able to research the invisible spiritual world, history was revealed as consisting entirely of the deeds of very 'concrete' spiritual beings, who are either incarnate (i.e. human beings) or disincarnate, such as dead human beings, and other spiritual beings of different levels of consciousness who have never been incarnate on the physical plane. He was able to describe how history has been affected by the balance between freedom in the actions of individual human beings and of necessity in the actions of mighty disincarnate spiritual beings whose actions involve thousands and millions of people. He showed how the destiny of some human beings, incarnate on the physical plane, worked consciously or unconsciously with disincarnate ones.

According to Steiner's spiritual research, which he constantly encouraged people to prove for themselves by the exercise of their healthy rational faculties, we can observe how different parts of the human spiritual-physical organism have been developed in different epochs of history. We are now living in the fifth of what he called the seven post-Atlantean epochs, each of which lasts 2160 years (2160 years is the length of time it takes the vernal equinox to 'precess' through one sign of the zodiac; the vernal equinox precesses 1° every 72 years). This fifth epoch began in AD 1413 and will continue until 3573. In the third and fourth epochs, man's life of feeling and thinking were developed respectively. In our fifth epoch, which he termed the Age of the Consciousness Soul, or Spiritual Soul, the decisive issue will be whether man can turn his new-found powers of individual thinking to serve the Good out of his own free choice or whether, encouraged by mighty spiritual adversary forces that exist to test man, he will use his powers of thought merely to satisfy the cravings of his own egotism and, in so doing, actively shut himself off from the positive forces of the spiritual world. The third epoch (2907 BC – 747 BC) was concerned with the polarity of beauty and ugliness, and morality was anchored in the experience of that polarity. The fourth epoch (747 BC – AD 1413) was the age of the polarity of truth and untruth in which morality was judged in the light of that polarity. Our own epoch will witness the struggle between good and evil in the human soul, not in any codified didactic sense, determined for all by spiritual authorities such as the Church, but now as a matter of conscience to be weighed and decided by each individual.

The nature of evil

In our time Rudolf Steiner has thrown great light on the problem of good and evil, and the meaning of evil in relation to the development of human freedom, especially in the post-Renaissance era. In particular, he showed how the traditional Church picture of a single adversary, alternatively called Satan, Lucifer or the Devil, is confused and inaccurate – the product of decadent and dysfunctional spiritual faculties – and that we have in fact to do with two Beings, who challenge man in two fundamentally different ways.

In the two remarkable buildings he designed and caused to be built in Dornach, Switzerland (the first was destroyed by arson on New Year's Eve 1922; the second still survives), Steiner placed a colossal wooden statue carved by himself and an English assistant Edith Maryon. The statue, which he named the Representative of Man, shows a Christlike figure standing between the two opposing spiritual Beings who seek to block man's development: the one, to whom Steiner referred by the ancient Persian name of Ahriman and whom he maintained corresponds to the biblical Satan, tries to persuade man that there is no existence other than the material and works to fetter man in the coldblooded abstractions of materialism; the other, for whom he used the traditional name of Lucifer (the biblical Devil), wishes to draw man away from earthly life altogether in hotheaded

Rudolf Steiner's wooden sculpture, 'The Group', with Lucifer (left) and Ahriman (below)

passions and egotistical illusions. Before the Incarnation of Christ, Lucifer was man's main adversary. The temptations of this Being can be felt especially in the ancient cultures and religions of Asia, but still today everywhere when an excess of zealous enthusiasm threatens to overpower the human soul. Since the Event of Palestine, and especially since the Renaissance, Ahriman, the Spirit of Materialism, has replaced Lucifer, the Spirit of Otherworldliness, as the main danger to humanity. His influence can be experienced notably in the cold abstractions of modern western science, in the frigidities of the law courts, and in the lies and half-truths propagated by the media. Lucifer's temptations are still with us, but he is a slowly fading power, who is forced to give ground to Ahriman. Before the Incarnation of Christ, by contrast, Ahriman's influence was gradually growing within humanity, but was still less than that of Lucifer. Both in time and in space, the Event of Palestine can be seen as the axial point of human history, for in general it can be said that Asian cultural development has primarily represented a struggle between luciferic forces and those spiritual forces which work for the good of humanity, while European and western development since Christ has primarily seen a struggle between those beneficent forces and the powers of Ahriman. In the millennia before Christ, Asia was the cradle of civilization, the vanguard of human development; Europeans were by contrast undeveloped peoples. After Palestine, the balance of human development shifted slowly from Asia to Europe. Asian cultures learned much from luciferic wisdom in the struggle against it. Western culture has to struggle against the seductions of Ahriman, and to learn from him without being ensnared by him.[2]

The incarnations of three cosmic Beings

Christ's physical Incarnation in Palestine, the spiritual centre of the world in the post-Atlantean epoch, in the body of Jesus of Nazareth, Steiner affirmed, was the fulcrum and central turning-point of all human evolution from the original creation of man in a non-physical state to man's eventual return in a non-physical state to the Godhead.[3] The Resurrection of Christ marked the end of man's incarnation into physical reality and *the very beginning* of his excarnation out of it. This is why Christ was so much more than just a moral teacher, as many of today's pundits argue He was. It was His Deed that was more important than His teaching. By identifying with man at the lowest level of human evolution—physicality—and by going through death and transcending it, He redirected the whole course of human development.

But since the essence of human development is bound up with the struggle for freedom, and that in turn with the question of the choice between good and evil, it was also necessary that the two Adversaries, Lucifer and Ahriman, should also incarnate on the physical plane at a particular time in human development.[4] Lucifer did so in the third millennium BC in China. The result of his incarnation was a mighty impulse given to the growth of individual human intellect, which led to new developments in government, in art, and the crafts. Steiner indicated that the whole glorious development of culture and art from ancient China to classical Greece cannot be understood without taking into account the impulse given by the incarnation of Lucifer. Soon after the beginning of the third millennium AD the balance between the three cosmic powers of Lucifer, Christ and Ahriman requires that Ahriman too will incarnate onto the physical plane—this time in the West, in America. Ahriman will also bring 'gifts' to man—gifts of a tremendous intellectual brilliance, gifts which will not emphasize man's egocentric individuality, as Lucifer's did, but ones which seduce man into thinking of himself only as part of a collective mass bound by birth and death to the material world. Just as Asia was the main scene of the unfolding of Lucifer's gifts, so the American continent will be—indeed already is—the main site where Ahriman's gifts will be laid before mankind. For this world-historical reason, and not on account of any ethnic prejudice against Americans, Rudolf Steiner frequently warned, especially in his later years, against the dangers of what he called 'Americanism'. By this he meant no blanket condemnation of American culture and society, but rather, the way in which Ahriman has been able to inject a particularly virulent form of materialism into American society, a materialism that in the twentieth century has increasingly 'blanketed' the world with its uniformity. This is no mere philosophical materialism, but a materialism of the will, of action, that directly affects the ways in which we live our lives.

Each of these mighty spiritual interventions in history have had to be long prepared, and that includes the land in which they are to take place and the people who live in that land: the Chinese, the Jews, the Americans. History has already speeded up since the death of Rudolf Steiner in 1925; he did not foresee the rapidity with which atomic power would become available for human use, for example, although he pointed to its eventual emergence. This unnatural acceleration is itself the result of the increasing pace of the preparations being made for Ahriman's incarnation, which is now imminent. The task for us is to live without dread through this mighty experience in full consciousness of what Ahriman brings and what needs to be done to counterbalance his coming.

Only by preserving a balance in the soul between these two mighty spiritual Beings, Lucifer and Ahriman, which is possible by relating to the power of the Christ, can man turn the one-sidedness of these Beings—cold ahrimanic intellect and passionate luciferic zeal—to humanity's advantage. Steiner's awesomely dynamic sculpture shows the Representative of Humanity acting out of a calm centre mastering the two by conscious recognition of them both in their respective domains. When they are seen, they are unable to steal into the soul and dominate it; but if they are unrecognized by the human ego, they can bend the soul to their will. They drive the ego off the stage of its own self-consciousness and act in its place.

For free moral choices to be possible, for humanity as a whole to be able to choose the good and the wholesome, there must be this formidable twofold opposition to healthy human development, and the destiny of some human beings has involved them, either for longer or shorter periods, with one or the other, and sometimes with both, of the forces of spiritual opposition. For example, Steiner indicated how certain brotherhoods in different countries and cultural regions, working out of profoundly occult and spiritual purposes of a malign nature, have sought to block the healthy development of humanity. These brotherhoods have served either luciferic or ahrimanic forces: in Asia, primarily luciferic forces; in the West, mainly ahrimanic ones. They are most certainly aware of each other. In lectures given in October 1915, Rudolf Steiner illustrated their interrelationships for example in their struggle for control over the Russian theosophical medium H.P. Blavatsky.[5]

Occult interference in world politics

Both before and during the First World War, Rudolf Steiner made a number of references to secret circles or brotherhoods in the West, notably in the British Empire and in America but also in France. These had a certain conception of the development of the twentieth century and were striving to realize that conception. Steiner referred, for example, in his lecture of 4 December 1916 at Dornach, Switzerland, to 'instruction [of the members of those brotherhoods] by means of maps which showed how Europe was to be changed' by the coming world war (the

First and Second World Wars) for which the brotherhoods were preparing.[6] In encountering such statements, the question arose in me: *if, as Steiner affirms, these brotherhoods were working in accordance with long-range plans that would affect world history beyond the twentieth century, had these groups remained active throughout the century, and could signs of their influence and activity be discerned in the public domain from Steiner's time until today?* This is the central question upon which this book is based. If such groups and their plans exist, and if events can be shown to have developed to some extent in accordance with their plans, then certain conclusions inevitably follow: first, that conventional academic explanations of modern historical events which take no account of such brotherhoods and their intentions are obviously inadequate; and second, that as long as society at large remains ignorant of such groups and their activities, it will continue to be manipulated by them.

My studies have convinced me that the answer to the central question posed above is in the affirmative. In addition to the work of Rudolf Steiner, I came across the writings of several men of insight who pointed clearly to the existence of groups which have sought influence in western society in order to realize profound and secretive historical aims. One such was C.G. Harrison, an Anglo-Catholic thinker and independent practitioner of theoretical occultism (i.e. of the 'pure' principles of occultism as distinct from the 'applied' technique of occultism, which is magic). In six lectures which he gave to members of the Berean Society — an association of 'Christian esotericists' — in London in 1893 as a High Church Anglican response to what he regarded as the dangerous new gnostic heresy of H.P. Blavatsky's theosophy, he outlined in the course of his exposition of the 'law of correspondence' the occult political principles underlying European history as well as something of the intentions of conflicting occult brotherhoods, some of them self-serving.[7]

Carroll Quigley   *Alfred Lord Milner*

Cecil Rhodes

How such ideas came to be realized in practice, on the political plane, for instance, can be gleaned from the work of Prof. Carroll Quigley (1910–77), who taught at the School of Foreign Service, Georgetown University, at Harvard and at Princeton. In two remarkable books, *The Anglo-American Establishment* (1949) and *Tragedy and Hope* (1966)[8] Quigley describes in considerable detail the secret society that emerged from the activities of Cecil Rhodes and his associates in the 1890s, and how it had insinuated itself into the Anglo-American establishment by the end of the First World War, after which it covertly directed the course of Anglo-American foreign policy and hence of much world politics until about 1945. In *Tragedy and Hope* (p.950) Quigley writes:

> I know of the operations of this network because I have studied it for 20 years and was permitted for two years, in the early 1960s, to examine its papers and secret records. [!] I have no aversion to it or to most of its aims and have, for much of my life, been close to it and to many of its instruments. I have objected, both in the past and recently, to a few of its policies ... but in general my chief difference of opinion is that it wishes to remain unknown, and I believe its role in history is significant enough to be known.

In his earlier book *The Anglo-American Establishment*, he expressed himself more strongly:

> In general, I agree with the goals and aims of the Milner Group. I feel that the British way of life and the British Commonwealth of Nations are among the great achievements of all history ... But agreeing with the Group on goals, I cannot agree with them on methods ... their lack of perspective in critical moments, their failure to use intelligence and common sense, their tendency to fall back on standardized social reactions and verbal clichés in a

crisis, their tendency to place power and influence into hands chosen by friendship rather than merit, their oblivion to the consequences of their actions, their ignorance of the point of view of persons in other countries or of persons in other classes in their own country . . .[9]

President Bill Clinton was groomed for the presidency by Averell Harriman and his wife Pamela, two of the very Establishment people Quigley wrote about, and was taught by Quigley himself at Georgetown. Clinton paid homage to his teacher in his 1992 Democratic Party nomination speech. Of the power exercised by what he called 'the secret society of Cecil Rhodes' and later, 'the Milner Group', Quigley wrote:

When the influence which the Institute [The Royal Institute of International Affairs, Chatham House] wields is combined with that controlled by the Milner Group in other fields — in education, in administration, in newspapers and periodicals — a really terrifying picture begins to emerge. This picture is called terrifying not because the power of the Milner Group was used for evil ends. It was not. On the contrary, it was generally used with the best intentions in the world [we recall that Quigley declared himself in agreement with the basic aims of the Group]. The picture is terrifying because such power . . . is too much to be safely entrusted safely to any one group . . . No country that values its safety should allow what the Milner Group established in Britain — that is, that a small number of men should be able to wield such power in administration and politics, should be given almost complete control over the publication of the documents relating to their actions, should be able to exercise such influence over the avenues of information that create public opinion, and should be able to monopolize so completely the writing and the teaching of the history of their own period.[10]

Quigley's evidence for the power wielded by Rhodes's secret society and its successors covers the period up to 1945. From his work it is clear that any study which ignores the influence of this secretive Anglo-American group from the 1890s until the middle of the twentieth century simply is not in touch with reality. But what of the second half of the twentieth century? At the end of *The Anglo-American Establishment* Quigley almost laments: 'It would seem that the great idealistic adventure which began with Toynbee and Milner in 1875 had slowly ground its way to a finish of bitterness and ashes.'[11] Was this the case? Did the occult purposes working through these particular political and cultural instruments suddenly cease simply because of the election of the Labour Government in 1945, as Quigley implies? Can their subsequent influence be detected today at the end of the twentieth century?

Again, my research leads me to answer this second question in the affirmative. What Quigley called 'the Milner Group' has not given up or gone away. To show the continuity with which their intentions have been maintained throughout this century, this book will examine in detail maps and articles which, I believe, reveal something of the occult aims of those who have shaped much of the development of the twentieth century and are even now seeking to dominate that of the twenty-first.

The book is offered in the spirit of watchfulness. It behoves us at this time of colossal historical change to be as awake as possible to the strategies and tactics of the adversaries of human progress. I realize that some of the interpretations in the book would not constitute 'proof' by normal legal or academic historical standards — they might be termed 'merely circumstantial'. However, I would invite readers simply to consider what is put forward, to compare it with what they know and, if interested, to do their own research to take things further.

1. Truth goes to the Hypnotist

Arthur Polzer-Hoditz was chief of staff to the last Habsburg Emperor Karl (1916–18). He wrote a book about his former master entitled *Kaiser Karl* ('Emperor Charles', Zurich-Leipzig-Vienna 1928). His brother Ludwig was a student of Rudolf Steiner's and knew Rudolf Steiner personally. From him we discover that Arthur Polzer-Hoditz obviously considered that something of the intentions of the western brotherhoods was contained in a map which, as he says, 'was published by the Englishman [Henry] Labouchère [MP] in his satirical weekly journal *Truth* in 1890 (the Christmas number dated 25 December 1890, not the regular number for that week which is also dated 25 December), that is, 24 years before the outbreak of the World War.' This map is reproduced on the frontispiece of this book. Polzer-Hoditz notes that the map is 'virtually identical with that of present-day Europe [i.e. of the 1920s], Austria as a monarchy has disappeared ... Bohemia is an independent state in the incidental shape of Czechoslovakia. Germany is squeezed into her [1920s] confines and split into small republics', and Russia is a 'Russian desert'.[1] Let us consider the map's other features, always remembering that it appeared in 1890 and was looking ahead to the new post-war Europe.

First, all states have become republics. Spain and Portugal are united, though there was no sign that this was even a remote possibility between 1890 and 1914. France, Italy and Switzerland seem to be unchanged from their 1890 borders and, surprisingly, Germany still seems to retain Alsace-Lorraine. Britain too is a republic, but we note that whereas Spain and Portugal are shown by one colour and their former border is missing, three colours are used to represent Ireland, Scotland and England/Wales. The term

'British Republic' is written diagonally so that it covers
Northern Ireland, but not present-day Eire. There was
sufficient space to have written it horizontally, but the
designer obviously chose not to do so.[2] Sweden and
Norway, which were united under one crown in 1890,
remain united but as a republic. This is interesting in view
of the fact that a Norwegian nationalist movement was well
under way in the last quarter of the nineteenth century, and
in fact Norway became independent from Sweden in 1905.
Denmark seems to have reverted to its larger pre-1864
border with Germany, but this may be because it was too
small to show properly, and Holland and Belgium are not
shown, perhaps for the same reason. Alternatively, it may
be that these three countries did not loom large in the plans
of the map's designers.

Germany at first sight seems to be smaller and is indeed
'split into small republics', as Polzer-Hoditz says, but it is
not quite clear how far its eastern border extends. He says
that it has been squeezed into 'its present confines' (the
German original has 'seine heutigen engen Grenzen' — its
present narrow borders), but the words 'German republics'
only extend as far as the eastern border of present-day
Germany, although the blue seems to include Silesia, which
Germany was forced to cede to Poland in 1945. If the orange
(Pomerania, west Prussia) and pink (east Prussia) are also
supposed to be German republics, then the size of Germany
as a whole has not decreased and Polzer-Hoditz is wrong.
Certainly, the new small Polish republic corresponds only
to the size of Russian Poland (as it was in 1890) and does not
appear to have the outlet to the sea that it was given after
1919. Note, however, that the area of blue does in fact
correspond to a considerable portion of what later became
Communist East Germany after 1945. Could the fact that
the orange and pink areas are not included under the name
'German republics' mean that they were destined for
severance from Germany? It is at least noteworthy that east

Prussia, which was separated off from the rest of Germany 1919–39 by the Polish corridor has a colour of its own. Note also that south-western Germany (Baden and Baden-Württemberg) also has its own colour (reddish) while the bulk of what was to become West Germany after 1945 is coloured a uniform orange. The key point about Germany in the map, then, is not so much the fact that it has shrunk overall—it has not (it even appears to have retained Alsace-Lorraine!)—but rather, that it has been split up into smaller republics.

Independent Bohemia (green) is not as large as Czecho-slovakia in the 1920s, as Polzer-Hoditz states; in fact it is not even named, but again, this may have been for reasons of space. Certainly, the fact that it is coloured green and not red like the neighbouring Austrian republic indicates that it was to be separated off from Austria. The Austrian repub-lic, for its part, seems to have grown; for although it has lost Bohemia it has retained the Tyrol (actually lost to Italy after the War), and has gained Bosnia-Hercegovina (annexed 1908), all of the territory of Yugoslavia and even Greece! In 1890, Greece, Serbia, and Montenegro were independent kingdoms. Bosnia-Hercegovina had been administered by Austria (with the agreement of the Great Powers) since the Congress of Berlin 1878, but was not yet formally annexed by Austria. Again, it could be that Greece, Serbia, etc., were not so significant in the long-range plans of the map's designers, although of course the Balkans were to play a vital instrumental role in bringing about war in 1914. It is noteworthy in this connection that the Turks do not figure at all on the map. The Ottoman Empire, which Britain had been supporting for decades against Russian ambitions, still held a considerable area of the Balkan peninsula in 1890, but in 1895 the Prime Minister, Lord Salisbury, indicated to the Kaiser his willingness to see the Ottoman Empire partitioned. The First Balkan War of 1912 was fought to eject the Turks from the Balkans and largely succeeded.[3]

Romania seems to have been incorporated into Bulgaria, the blue area of which even extends as far north as Galicia (in 1890 part of the Austro-Hungarian Empire) and almost as far as the Crimea. Russia has therefore lost territory to Bulgaria. What this could mean is not so clear, but one fact stands out, namely, that whereas in 1890 Russia had direct borders with Germany and Austria-Hungary, the map shows that Russia has been cut off from the Germanic nations by a corridor of intermediaries: Bulgarian blue, Polish red, and east Prussian pink (assuming that east Prussia is no longer German, and indeed, since 1945, it has not been). We shall return to this point later.

Lastly, Russia itself, over which Tsar Alexander III ruled in 1890, does not even bear the word 'republic'; it has become a 'desert'. Why will be discussed later in considering the context of the map. The three Baltic republics, Estonia, Latvia and Lithuania, for which, in 1890, there was no prospect of the independence they were to obtain in 1918, remain subsumed in Russia, while Finland, for which there was equally little prospect, despite a growing nationalist movement there, has become an independent republic.

What does the map reveal?

The map therefore contains a number of anomalies and surprises. The key changes, however, are those affecting Germany and Russia. Where the map's 'predictions' were borne out was in the emergence after the First World War of the republics of Finland and Poland, the reduction (?) of Germany, the enlargement of Bulgaria (but not by nearly so much), and Austria's loss of Bohemia and Galicia. In addition, Germany and Austria did indeed become republics. But many countries which the map says were to turn republican after the War did not, and various other features of the post-1919 situation are absent. Is one then justified in seeing this map as having anything to do with the plans of the western brotherhoods, as Polzer-Hoditz did?

The answer is yes, for a number of reasons. First, the fact that the map 'got some things wrong' is not so significant in itself. Rudolf Steiner pointed to various examples of 'intervention' in human history by both the beneficent and maleficent spiritual powers which did not succeed, or only partially succeeded.[4] Despite the insidious and forceful way in which the opposing powers operate — assassinations are a prime example — they are often frustrated by the deeds of human beings working consciously or unconsciously in the service of the Higher Hierarchies. Also, it may be that since the being which Steiner called Ahriman often tends to work through half-truths rather than outright lies, the map is a deliberate combination of 'fact' and fancy, between which the careful observer has to discriminate.

This brings us to an important point. If the western brotherhoods are clandestine, why would they advertise their intentions in a weekly journal sold in ordinary shops? As Rudi Lissau wrote in the journal *Anthroposophy Today* (No. 11, Autumn 1990, p.37), 'secret societies are secret and usually manage to remain so'. In other words, they do not advertise their existence and their plans. But this may not always be the case. It is often said that 'the criminal feels a need to return to the scene of the crime'. Might it not also be that the criminals, in this case those occult brotherhoods more or less consciously serving the forces of opposition, do in fact advertise their crimes *before* they commit them? Could it not be that the media, for instance, are used by such powers in two ways — both to pull the wool over the eyes of ordinary folk, who may not even be aware of such goings-on, and also to *inform* their agents and subconscious sympathizers throughout society — those who can actually read the signs and those who 'feel' them — of the brotherhoods' intentions? Rudolf Steiner himself drew people's attention to the forecasts of the assassination of the Austrian Crown Prince which appeared in the Parisian journal *Almanach de Mme de Thebes*, 1½ years before the murder.[5]

The Japanese have two expressions which might help to understand this point about the brotherhoods 'advertising' their intentions. The first is *nemawashi* — digging round the roots. Before a businessman, for example, presents any proposal to a meeting, he holds discreet meetings with each of the individuals he expects to be at the meeting and gains their support beforehand. At the meeting itself, his proposal then goes through on the nod with the minimum of fuss or opposition. The second expression is *fun'iki zukuri* — creating an atmosphere. If a politician or party wishes to bring about a certain outcome which society will accept as a *de facto* event, they need to be first subconsciously and then later consciously convinced of its inevitability. You do not simply put forward your idea, saying 'this must happen'. You approach it obliquely from various angles and through various media. You saturate the social atmosphere with a more or less conscious expectation of the event, and then, when everyone is ready to accept it, you bring it consciously forward, and hey presto, it is accepted almost as a matter of course.

The Kaiser's progress

To understand more about the intentions behind the *Truth* map of 1890, it will be necessary to look at the contexts in which the map appeared: the illustration and the related article of which it is a part, the magazine in which it appeared, and the historical background to the appearance of the article. First, some observations about the illustration to which the map belongs. It purports to show a dream in which the young Kaiser (31 years old in 1890) sees his whole life before him. The events around the Kaiser's head show his past up to 1890 in six episodes: 1) His boyhood. 2)

Doctors arguing over his father's deathbed. A liberal-minded man married to the equally liberally-minded English Princess Victoria, daughter of Queen Victoria, Kaiser Frederick III died of cancer of the throat in 1888 after only three months on the throne. His German doctors suspected his English specialist physician Dr Morell Mackenzie, sent by Queen Victoria's advisors, of failing to save the Kaiser's life. The German doctors had called for an operation, but were overruled by Mackenzie who declared the cancer benign. Mackenzie proved to be wrong; Frederick succumbed in June 1888 and the last chance for a liberal anglophile Emperor of Germany disappeared. 3) Queen Victoria making off with his father's diary, and the Kaiser berating Victoria (and her son, the Prince of Wales, later Edward VII) for doing such a thing (this episode is shown in three scenes). On Frederick's death, his wife immediately sent his diaries to her mother in England. Wilhelm bitterly resented his mother's action. 4) Wilhelm II's argument with Bismarck which led to the Chancellor's resignation in March 1890. 5) Wilhelm's efforts to please both the monarchs of Europe and 6) the workers of Germany. 7) The scene shifts the action to the future. He sees his popularity outstripped by that of Bismarck; the people will not love him. 8) Radicals attempt revolution. 9) He tries to overawe the people by recourse to war with Russia. 10) Defeated, he returns, Napoleon-like. 11) He goes to England, only to be scolded by Victoria and the other monarchs. 12) He sees the end of the European monarchies caused by his own folly. 13) The *deus ex machina* — he beholds the map of the new republican Europe.

Before turning from the illustration to the article to which it belongs, one notes the Kaiser in the bottom left-hand corner standing on the French tricolour. This is where he resolves to go to war with Russia. Then in the scene above where he is pleading with Victoria, we see the Prince of Wales (later Edward VII, 1901–10) next to her. Beside him is

the Tsar Alexander III (1881–94), and on his right, Emperor
Franz Josef of Austria-Hungary (1848–1916). The latter two,
both arch-conservative monarchs, can be recognized by
their distinctive beards, their crowns and the double eagles
surmounting them. In the last scene, Alexander and Franz
Josef enter the workhouse, accompanied by what looks like
two of the monarchs from the previous sketch. Lastly,
between the scene of the workhouse and the map of the new
order is a red Phrygian cap, the symbol of republicanism
and revolution not so much of the early twentieth century
as of the period of the French Revolution. Jacobinism and
Freemasonry were regarded as the ultimate enemies by the
continental monarchs of the nineteenth century. The
Phrygian cap is the symbol of the anti-monarchical anti-
aristocratic republicanism of the French Revolution and is
inextricably associated with France. The illustration therefore alludes twice to France, or three times if one includes
the Kaiser's Napoleon-like retreat from Russia. These allusions to France should be kept in mind.

Hypnotism and the Kaiser's dream

The article, or rather story, in which the map appeared was
carried in a special Christmas issue of the satirical weekly
magazine, *Truth* (somewhat similar to *Private Eye*), and bore
the date 25 December 1890. Christmas Day, the birth of light
in the darkness, the coming of a new impulse. What this
new impulse was will be evident in due course. Rudolf
Steiner indicated that Ahriman, the adversary of human
spiritual progress, would work especially through writers,
many of great brilliance, such as Friedrich Nietzsche. One
could well imagine that not a few of these scintillating
minds would find their way into the media, and it is particularly the lack of a sense for truth on which Rudolf
Steiner focused in the lectures of late 1916.[6] The Christmas
issue of 1890 was built around a single theme — the fad of

hypnotism, 'The Very Latest "Ism"'. It was in fact the fifteenth 'ism' to have entertained society, according to *Truth*.
All the others will not be named here, but it can be pointed
out that the first 'ism' mentioned was Unionism, the
seventh was Spiritualism, and the fourteenth was Theo-
sophism. Each of the 'isms' was subjected to lampooning in
the form of a 15-line verse, each of which ended with the
refrain:

> (Theosophism) bored/bragged/boomed/cursed etc. its
> last and died.

Hypnotism, however, says *Truth*, 'now holds the field ...
'midst persons of all classes, from the Monarch to the
masses' and it

> *isn't fated yet to pass and die.* [Emphasis added]
>   No, Hypnotical experiment
>   Will induce much further merriment
> Before it is its fate to pass and die!'

Truth is not only the name of the journal, but also of its
symbol, a Grecian nymphlike creature, and she resolves to
investigate the new craze by hiring a Professor of hypnotism to teach her how it is done.

> In short, 'twas her hope to join work and diversion
>   By exerting around her hypnotic coercion.

She told the professor that she longed to possess his
remarkable power:

> For placed as I am, I am certain 'twould be,
> Every day of the week, of assistance to me.

She assured him she would use the power responsibly:

> Not to laughter provoke and amusement to cause,
> Or to gain, to no purpose, diurnal applause,

> But to aid me in schemes I have mused upon long,
> For suppressing abuses I know to be wrong;

The Professor quickly realizes that this is no ordinary pupil:

> ... you possess in full degree the power we call hypnotic,
> And if you your strong will exert
> You all around you will assert
> An influence despotic.

(N.B. This was six years before the beginning of popular mass journalism, which began in 1896 with the publication of Northcliffe's *Daily Mail*.) The professor instructs her that there are three hypnotic powers. Power no. 1, which he sketches very briefly, makes subjects obey the hypnotist's will. Power no. 2, described in a little more detail, but still very sketchily, forces subjects to speak and carry out whatever they are thinking. Power no. 3 enables the hypnotist to read another's thoughts at a distance. What is portrayed here, then, is a threefoldness relating to thinking, speaking and willing in which the hypnotist progressively takes command of the subject's inner life. Furthermore, the first power relates hypnotist and subject at the level of action; the focus is on the hypnotist. This is the kind of hypnosis with which most people are perhaps familiar. In the case of the second and third powers, the subject is more the focus; the hypnotist simply observes.

Interestingly enough, *Truth* immediately opts for the third power, declaring: 'I'd like to know the present thoughts of the young German Kaiser.' She does not say why of all things she wants this first, especially since she had told the professor that she wanted his power 'to aid me in schemes I have mused upon long, For suppressing abuses I know to be wrong.' Nor does she explain her reason after she has finished with the Kaiser. He is in the middle of a dream, and it is this—in the form of 15 stanzas of eight or nine lines each—that the map and accompanying scenes illustrate. In a brief speech before the dream proper, the Kaiser says:

> Pictures of my past existence first obtruded with persistence;
> Then as in a magic mirror, I've my future seen displayed;
> Seen my coming life depicted, and such wrongs on me inflicted,
> That, as I've already told you, I am sad and sore afraid.

After relating his failure to impress his people, and their subsequent attempts at revolution, he says:

> One course alone was left me
>   My prestige to regain —
> *To war with Russia I'd to go,*
> With pomp, and panoply, and show [emphasis added]

Then, following his defeat at the hands of the Russians and his humiliation in England, he describes how, 'hoarsely cursing my fatal love of gore' the Kings of Europe one by one 'hobbled in through the workhouse door!' Then follow the last two stanzas:

> Then from the wall before me
>   There slowly was unrolled
> A brand-new map of Europe,
>   On which, in type of gold,
> I read how Kings and Kaisers
>   Had wholly passed away,
> In the effulgent sunlight
>   Of democratic day!
>
> Yes; sick at heart I studied
>   That renovated map,
> With its allied Republics,
>   The fruit of my mishap!
> And as 'Potz-tausend Teufel!'

From me in fury broke,
Your summons, TRUTH, aroused me,
    And with a start I woke!

Truth declares herself 'terrified greatly' by what she has seen: 'I shall certainly not use my Power number three', she says, giving no reason why not, but wishes to learn how to use the others without delay. Finally, the Professor says to her, after casting various spells:

Your weird and occult power
    Latent too long, is yours to use from this
auspicious hour – [emphasis added]

Truth immediately goes to visit the Prime Minister Lord Salisbury, who happens to be in discussions with the German Ambassador when she arrives. She discovers that Salisbury too has hypnotic powers, of which he says:

So by luck I developed that power
    Which seems on the mystic to border
And it's thanks to the force
    I've derived from that source
That I've kept all my colleagues in order.

There follows a list of all the Ministers of State claimed to be 'hypnotized' by Salisbury. Apart from these seemingly innocuous remarks, *Truth* gleans little else from the Prime Minister, so she goes to Marlborough House to meet the Prince of Wales:

'I've come,' said *Truth*, to ask you if it's true
A power hypnotic now belongs to you?
Rumour asserts that you've acquired it lately
And used it, too, unless report errs greatly,
In making people do the oddest acts;
Pray tell me then if these are actual facts?'

'They are,' returned the Prince, 'For sometime past
I have been under training, and at last
Am able, as you have already heard
To make folks do things utterly absurd.'

Subsequent conversation with the Prince reveals little of interest, however, and this completes the survey of the map, its article and the magazine. It is worth pointing out, however, that precisely these two individuals — Salisbury and the Prince of Wales (who, from 1874 until his accession as King Edward VII in 1901, was Grand Master of Britain's Freemasons[7]) were, according to the historian Renate Riemeck, the leaders of the cabal of powerful figures in the British establishment that carried out a long-term and ultimately successful plan to effect a diplomatic revolution that would lead to the encirclement of Germany and was aimed at precipitating the First World War.[8] We shall turn now to the historical context in which the map appeared and consider the phenomena of the map and article against that background.

The meaning of the Illustrations

The first question to ask about the illustrations around the map is: why is the Kaiser standing on the French flag? France was Germany's worst potential enemy at the time, since she burned with revenge for the defeat inflicted by Prussia in the war of 1870–71. Bismarck's diplomacy had mainly been aimed at securing Germany's defence against any such revanchist ambitions. It might therefore seem natural that the Kaiser is shown standing on the tricolour, except that in the 15-stanza satirical verse that accompanies this illustration there is no mention of France or any suggestion that France would be involved in a Russo-German war. It might alternatively be thought that the Kaiser is standing on the French flag as a gesture of his distaste for

Robert Cecil, Marquess of Salisbury, Prime Minister 1885–86, 1886–92, 1895–1902

Albert Edward, Prince of Wales (later King Edward VII, r. 1901–10), Grand Master of British Freemasonry 1874–1901, Grand Protector of the Order 1901–10

the revolutionaries shown in the previous scene which he seems to be looking at. But the stanza relating to that scene says:

> And fired upon and hooted,
>   Whilst prancing through the street
> I had (my vision showed me)
>   To rapidly retreat!

In other words, the Kaiser was one of the figures on horseback shown in the previous scene being fired upon by the revolutionaries; he was not watching the revolutionaries. If it is objected that he could be standing on the flag because he was remembering his humiliation of the previous scene and associating revolutionaries with France, the obvious rejoinder is why not then go to war with France, which in 1890 was without allies. Yet the Kaiser said in his dream, 'One course alone was left me,' namely, war with Russia. Why one course alone? Until March 1890 Germany had had a secret treaty with Russia, which von Caprivi, the Chancellor who followed Bismarck, failed to renew. Russia in December 1890 then was without allies, as were France and splendidly isolated Britain. Yet Germany and Russia, both autocracies, seemed to have far more in common than Russia and France, and the Kaiser and the Russian Crown Prince (later Nicholas II) were cousins. Relations between republican France and autocratic Russia, on the other hand, were severely strained and for them to become allies would have seemed fantastical to most people.

Nevertheless, as Renate Riemeck describes in her book, plans had been set in motion by the circle around the Prince of Wales as early as 1887 to bring France and Russia together in an alliance (which Britain would support at the crucial time) aimed at the defeat of the Central European allies, Germany and Austria.[9] Implausible as the trio of Britain, France and Russia might have seemed in 1887, the first stage of the plan was realized seven years later in 1894 when the Franco-Russian Dual Alliance became a reality. Negotiations between France and Russia had begun in July 1891, seven months after the map appeared in *Truth*. Two symbols of France, then, the French tricolour and the Phrygian cap of the French Revolution (not to mention the depiction of the Kaiser as Napoleon), appear almost incidentally in the map in connection with a war with Russia. The dream implies that the war will lead to the end of European monarchies, notably those of Russia, Austria and Germany, and to the creation of democracies all over Europe, all of which events the dream makes clear would be 'the fruit of my mishap', i.e. the Kaiser's war with Russia. How was it foreseen in 1890 that changes of such magnitude would result simply from an unlikely war between Germany and Russia? It is often said that the infamous alliance systems were responsible for the Europe-wide cataclysm of 1914, but in 1890 there was only one alliance — that between Germany, Austria-Hungary and Italy. Furthermore, relations between Britain and Germany were reasonably good in 1890, and Wilhelm was largely an unknown quantity, having been Emperor for only two years. Nevertheless, the map and those behind it had 'one course alone' plotted out for the hapless young 31-year-old Kaiser.

Riemeck cites czarist foreign ministry documents, first made public in 1932, which make clear that the process leading to the Franco-Russian Alliance had started in September 1887 when Lord Salisbury, a key member of Prince Edward's circle, and later Prime Minister and Foreign Minister from 1895 until 1902, met with the French diplomat Count Chaudordy and informed him of the plans for a Franco-Russian alliance.[10] In this context it may well be significant that in the midst of the pre-war crisis of 1914 a letter appeared in *The Times* on 1 August, three days before Britain entered the War by declaring war on Germany. Written by one MEMOR and giving no address, the letter read: 'Though Lord Salisbury died before the Anglo-French Agreement, it was carried through by the Minister who had held the seals of the Foreign Office under himself and by a Cabinet which was the continuation of his own and which was presided over by his nephew and political heir' (Arthur Balfour).

> So by luck I developed that power
>   Which seems on the mystic to border
> And it's thanks to the force
>   I've derived from that source
> That I've kept all my colleagues in order

Was it really only luck, we may ask?

Who's for the workhouse?

The next question relating to the map concerns those who do and those who do not enter the workhouse. Note that Tsar Alexander III enters first, followed by Franz Josef of Austria-Hungary—in other words, Russia, followed by Austria. This is of course what ultimately happened. Tsar Nicholas II abdicated in March 1917, and Franz Josef's successor, Kaiser Karl of Austria, followed in November 1918. Above all, it is significant that Victoria and Edward (i.e. Britain) are not shown entering the workhouse, although the map shows Britain as a republic, and the magazine's editor, Henry Labouchère, was a Radical politician who favoured republicanism. He nevertheless frequently hobnobbed with leading Tories, including Salisbury and the Prince. If the Prince were, in some sense, his superior, it would hardly do to show the Prince or his mother going into the workhouse. What then of his republicanism? Would that not have been an affront to the Prince?

Through his work with the Prince's Trust, his speeches, books and films which have stimulated many, both in

Britain and abroad, to think again about various social issues, Prince Charles has shown himself to be, like his forefather Prince Albert, someone who happens to be Crown Prince and who is attempting to serve the good in the station in which he finds himself in life.[11] One has the feeling that with such a man the fact of his royalty is really not as important as his character and what he is seeking to achieve. The same can surely be equally true on 'the other side', that is, one can be working against the ultimate interests of an institution like the monarchy and yet still be a member of it.

The active internationalist stream of American foreign policy has been carried as much, if not more, by Democrat administrations as by Republican since Woodrow Wilson's time. It is perfectly possible for Democrats and Republicans, or monarchists and republicans, to work together to achieve certain agreed aims. As Rudolf Steiner put it:

> ... there are higher instances, 'empires', which can quite well make use of both Masons and Jesuits in order to achieve what they want to achieve through the collaboration of the two. Do not believe that there can be no individuals who are not both Jesuit and Freemason. They have progressed beyond the point of working in one direction only. They know that it is necessary to tackle situations from various sides in order to push matters in a particular direction.[12]

This is a point frequently missed by those who cursorily dismiss the possibility of Freemasonry's involvement in far-reaching conspiracies, asserting that 'there were Freemasons on both sides of many conflicts, fighting against each other, as in the French Revolution, the Napoleonic Wars, the American Civil War, etc. To claim that Freemasons were commonly conspiring to bring about a certain end is therefore absurd.' People who make such arguments fail to realize that, while it may not have been the case that all Freemasons on both sides of a particular conflict were working towards the same end, to be able to place certain members of the same organization in key positions on both sides would obviously be a very effective strategy.[13]

The Russian 'desert'

The third, and possibly weightiest question, is: why the Russian 'desert'? Firstly, Russia was the victor in the Kaiser's dream, and the verse implies that Wilhelm's war against Russia is what leads Europe's monarchs to the workhouse, yet Alexander III is shown with his fellow monarchs berating Wilhelm II after the war is over. The map shows Russia as a 'desert' not a republic, so it might be thought that the Czar will continue to rule, but over a desert. However, all Europe's other states have become republics 'of democratic day' and the penultimate verse clearly says that 'Kings and Kaisers had wholly passed away'. It would seem then that Russia, despite winning the war against Germany, is to lose its czarist regime and become a desert, which is of course what happened after 1917 both on the material and spiritual levels. During and after the civil war of 1918–21, Russia was stricken by a terrible famine which had claimed some seven million lives by 1921, and Lenin's Bolsheviks were saved largely thanks to infusions of American money and food aid.[14] The Bolsheviks went on to create a spiritual desert through which the 'people of Christ', as Steiner calls the Russians,[15] had to wander for 70 years.

It was pointed out earlier that the map appeared at Christmas, the time of new birth. It was to herald a new era in more ways than one.

> Your weird and occult power
>   Latent too long, is yours to use from this
>   auspicious hour —

On hearing of the death of Wilhelm's grandfather, Kaiser Wilhelm I, in 1888, Lord Salisbury, who, it will be remembered, had already begun to put his plans into operation the year before, wrote enigmatically: 'This is the crossing of the bar. I see the sea covered with white horses.'[16] Wilhelm I was followed by his son, the liberal-minded Frederick III, who reigned for only three months before tragically dying of cancer of the throat in the prime of life. Thus it was that the young Wilhelm II became Emperor at the age of 29. The young, wilful and inexperienced Kaiser soon clashed with Prince Bismarck, Europe's master diplomat, and the dismissal of Bismarck in March 1890 led to a new era in European diplomacy, one that is known to both British and German historians as 'the New Course'.

The French were delighted to see their old enemy Bismarck out of the way, and immediately began to make approaches to the Russians. Meanwhile, that same year in November, the Vatican made a significant move in the direction of mending its fences with the French Third Republic, a regime it had always considered to be 'atheist and Freemasonic'. It did so, according to Riemeck, as part of its strategy for the twentieth century, which was to abandon the old alliance with aristocracy and embrace western democracy with a conservative Christian-democratic, i.e. Catholic-controlled, politics. A key figure in persuading the Vatican to help bring about a *rapprochement* between France and Russia was the Duke of Norfolk, Britain's pre-eminent Catholic aristocrat, another personal friend of Salisbury and member of the Prince's circle, who was sent to Rome in 1887 to let the Pope in on aspects of the British view of the twentieth century. The British intention, eagerly taken up by Leo XIII, was to have the Vatican act as the broker of the

Franco-Russian Alliance. This was another seemingly fantastical notion in say, 1880, but again one which eventually turned into reality.[17]

Why should the Prince's circle have sought to use the Vatican to join France and Russia in unholy diplomatrimony ('making people do the oddest acts')? Because in order to destroy something, to crack a nut, for example, one needs two forces, an active and a passive one, just as one needs two such forces to create a life: man, woman, and resulting baby. France, burning with lust for revenge, and egged on and aided by Britain, was to be the hammer; Russia, with its endless capacity for suffering, was to be the anvil. Between these two the Germanic nut was cracked in the First World War. On numerous occasions Rudolf Steiner spoke of the backward-looking impulses of the Papacy, inspired by the other major spiritual source of opposition to human progress, for which Rudolf Steiner used the traditional term Lucifer; this was not the first, nor would it be the last occasion when ahrimanic forces (the Prince's circle) cooperated with luciferic forces to achieve ends desirable to them both.[18]

And why? What was the intention of those whose influence may well have led to the appearance of this map? It was once well stated by Rudi Lissau:

> If it was the aim of a group of people to erect a dominion of materialism, an ahrimanic power structure, it was reasonable to make Germany a moral outcast, not because the country was utterly different from the rest of Europe, but because it was the birthplace of spiritual science ... [which] contained the seed of the threefold ordering of society, which would do away with ahrimanic power structures and market forces.[19]

Note that the map and the verse places the blame for the future war and upheaval squarely on the shoulders of the Kaiser (and by implication, Germany), already in 1890, when he was still largely an unknown factor! Yet by 1918, the notion of Germany's sole war guilt ('the most barbarous nation in the history of the world', etc. etc.) had become fixed in the minds of millions. This is in fact intimately related to the question of the Russian 'desert'.

Rudolf Steiner spoke many times of the vital importance for mankind's evolution of the development of a healthy relationship between Central and Eastern Europe.[20] What is at stake is the manner in which mankind passes from the fifth to the sixth post-Atlantean epoch, which is not destined to begin until AD 3573. In the present era of the development of the Consciousness Soul (the fifth post-Atlantean epoch), the Germanic peoples (who include, of course, Anglo-Saxons) have a crucial role to play, while in the coming era of the spirit-self humanity's vanguard will be the Slavic peoples. English-speaking culture particularly aids the process of emancipation from traditional instinctive ties of all kinds (blood, tribe, family, religion), and enables the personal, the individual, to emerge, but separate and alone. Germanic culture has within it spiritual qualities that enable the isolated individual to find the spiritual again within the self and thus rediscover a relationship, at first mainly in the realm of thought, with the spiritual world.

To this achievement of a light-filled Ego in the fifth epoch, Slavic culture in the sixth epoch will bring a Christ-inspired capacity for brotherhood, a truly transformed enwarmed life of feeling. The seeds of the sixth epoch are being laid now as humanity reaches the twenty-first century of the Christian era. Are those seeds to be healthy or diseased? That is one way of putting the question. The twenty-first century and the approach to it in the twentieth century are of tremendous importance, as was the ninth century, because just as the two 'ages' of 9 and 21 signify major milestones in the incarnation of the human ego, so do the eighth/ninth and twentieth/twenty-first centuries signify similar milestones in the progressive incarnation of humanity's Ego, the Christ, into the consciousness of humanity. To help humanity in this fifth epoch gain consciousness of its own Ego, which is the Cosmic Christ, the Etheric Christ — this was at the heart of Rudolf Steiner's anthroposophy, the wisdom of man.

Materialism and the English-speaking world

Constantly seeking to frustrate Christ's incarnation is the major Adversary in our time, Ahriman. In the fifth epoch, Ahriman is working particularly, though not exclusively, through powerful groups within English-speaking society and in those of its allies, notably Japan, because it is in Anglo-Saxon culture that the strongest impulses towards materialism lie in the modern world. Why the English-speaking world? To answer this question, it is first necessary to consider the geographical position of the British Isles. They lie at the westernmost edge of the Eurasian landmass. A glance at this vast area shows it to be a colossal triangle lying on its side with its base extending from the Bering Strait to Singapore. (In passing, it may be noted that the other continents, with the exception of Australia, are also triangles, wider in the north and tapering to points in the south.) Furthermore, the gesture of the coastline of East Asia is predominantly curvilinear. The opposite is the case in Europe, a continent compressed into a small area at the top of the Eurasian triangle and full of peninsulas and rectilinear forms.

These geographical features are reflected in the social and cultural forms of Eurasia. One can observe how in the East of the Eurasian triangle society has preserved essentially collective forms; there is a greater respect for tradition, for blood-lines, and for the invisible spiritual and elemental worlds. In Europe, by contrast, there has been greater emphasis on individualism and a greater breakdown of all traditional social forms, notably those depending on the blood. As materialism took hold in European culture after the Middle Ages, doubt and cynicism about any super-sensible or spiritual world increased; most Europeans today are historical materialists, even if not in the strictly Marxist sense of the term. Just as one can see a large-scale three-foldness in the Eurasian landmass as a whole, there is also a threefoldness within its parts. Within the Asian cultural area is Japan/China, India, the Middle East. And in the European cultural area is the Western European area (British Isles, Iberia, France), the Central European area (including Italy), and the Eastern European area (the Orthodox world).

It is no accident that it has been the Western Europeans (British, French, Spanish, Portuguese, Dutch, and Norwegians) who in the period 1500–1900 were the greatest world travellers and founders of empires; they are peoples who are more oriented to the outer world of the senses. The peoples of Eastern Europe, who paradoxically occupy the greater physical space, are those least preoccupied with the physical world of the senses; their main interest has been in the affairs of the soul and of the spirit, of religion and mysticism. All their politics, even in the modern era, has been profoundly linked with religion (many have commented on the religious aspects of Russian Communism, for instance). The peoples of Central Europe have been in the middle, between these outer and inner proccupations with the senses and with the spirit respectively. Among them, as a result, has developed most keenly the life of thought, of ideals, of philosophy, and also of music.

This threefolding within European culture has led the Western Europeans, especially the British, to develop the economic sphere, the Central Europeans the political sphere, and the Eastern Europeans the spiritual sphere. What marks the British out from the other Western Europeans, however, is not only the fact that the British Isles were under the direct influence of the Roman Empire and of the Papacy for a shorter period than France and Iberia, but also the fundamental fact that Britain is an island. 'No man is an island,' wrote John Donne in the early seventeenth century; 'I am a rock, I am an island,' sang Paul Simon in the late twentieth. To live on an island, where all speak the same language and share the same religion as oneself is to have a different consciousness from those who live on a continent where one's neighbours speak differently and have another religion. An islander is made aware of physical limits, and his sense of belonging to his national group is stronger and deeper than that of those who live in a world of shifting boundaries on a map. This is as true of Japan in the East as it is of Britain in the West. Unlike Japan, however, Britain is a geologically ancient land, firm and relatively stable. On the contrary, its climate is extremely changeable and unpredictable. These two factors have greatly enhanced the phlegmatic character of the British. Before they arrived in Britain, the Anglo-Saxons of Northern Germany and Jutland were already one of the more phlegmatic and earth-oriented groups of the larger Germanic race. The 'solidity' of temperament needed to deal with the changeable British weather made them more so. W.J. Stein, a student of Rudolf Steiner, pointed out that as time went by the British developed a special liking for the crystalline qualities of the salt carried on the winds that blew over them from the Atlantic.[21] They took this penchant for the crystalline and square into their diet (their toast, their desire for sugar, their potato crisps!); their architecture (the British were the first to develop the Decorated and Perpendicular styles of medieval architecture, the precursors of modern rectangular design, and to design their churches like castles); their music (they have a love of massed choral singing in block harmonies rather than flowing melodic lines); their military techniques (from ancient times they preferred to fight on foot, close to the earth, rather than on horseback, and later enemies came to fear their footsoldiers' squares); and Freemasonry, their own form of occultism, much of which is based on the square. All these elements contributed to the British, and especially the English, becoming a peculiarly 'grounded' people who in time moved naturally in the direction of empiricism and pragmatism, with a marked tendency to suspect anything idealistic, mystical and grandiose.

It was *these* Western Europeans and not the Spanish or the French who won the battle for North America and founded the United States. It was their stark solid Puritanism (boosted by that of their ancestors, the Low German Dutch) that provided much of the basis for American morality and religion. American culture, at least in its first 200 years (1620–1840), can indeed be described predominantly as an offshoot, an appendage even, of Britain. Furthermore, the American continent has its own spiritual quality which enhances the materialism of its British parent. Rudolf Steiner indicated that all mountain ranges running from north to south contain strong magnetic forces which tend to boost the magnetism within the human organism and thus strengthen the 'human double' within it.[22] This is an ahrimanic being which attaches itself to the organism of every human being soon after birth and flees it shortly before death. It lives within the electromagnetism of the human body, and it is the energy of this being, not of the real life force of the individual, that is measured by electrocardiograph machines and the like.

Ahriman and his servants in the western occult brotherhoods, together with their political 'frontmen', who are either conscious or unconscious of their service, have been striving since at least the early seventeenth century precisely to prevent the kind of 'spiritual communion' between Central and Eastern Europe that Steiner said was so important for humanity's future.[23] It is Central Europe that has the cultural task of nurturing the self-conscious 'I' of modern humanity in the fifth post-Atlantean epoch (1413–3573), and of defending the inner space in which this I can unfold, free of both the tendencies to spiritual authoritarianism and nebulous mysticism in the East and the aspiritual materialism and self-doubt of the West. In the fifth epoch man needs to learn to think spiritual thoughts and develop a spiritual imagination in full consciousness and out of his own free will.

Western European culture (especially the Anglo-American stream) will necessarily bring man to a 'free' (in the sense of no discernible external constraints) but isolated sense of self, a dangerous desert-like condition in which he can easily lose himself or even destroy himself out of despair or anomie; this represents the crucifixion of modern man on the cross of materialism. The Resurrection will come through the spiritualization of thinking, which is possible only in the inner sanctuary of the ego. In Rosicrucianism (seventeenth century), Goetheanism (eighteenth/nineteenth century and anthroposophy (twentieth century), Central European culture has provided the means for such a Resurrection of human thinking. These are all impulses which originated in Central Europe and which can help the Slavic peoples to form a relationship to the Christ which is a free deed of the ego and not one that is based on the instinctive consciousness of the past. The word 'isolation' is related to the word 'insulation'. Where Western European thinking isolates (makes individuals into islands; 'island' is *insula* in Latin), Central European culture has within it the power to reconnect the individual with the whole. The reconnected individual's spiritualized thinking will then be enhanced and 'enwarmed' by the thorough spiritualization of feeling which will be made possible in the sixth post-Atlantean epoch (3573–5733) through the Eastern European culture, notably the Russians.

In 1909 Rudolf Steiner began to speak of the momentous

reappearance of Christ in the etheric realm. He would become visible to more and more individuals, as He was to Paul before Damascus, as a result of humanity's unconscious crossing of the threshold of the spiritual world since 1900 and the return of powers of natural clairvoyance. This the Adversaries feared more than anything else, and so, in the 1930s, when, according to Rudolf Steiner, the Etheric Christ would begin to become visible to humanity, Hitler was enabled to emerge, in another bizarre example of cooperation between ahrimanic and luciferic forces. Much of Germany's spiritual energy was offered to Hitler instead of to Christ, while Stalin sought to capture that of Russia. Both men tempted their people with luciferic dreams of national 'spiritual' greatness which were made to serve ahrimanic plans for the complete mechanization and dehumanization of the German and Russian peoples. During the Second World War, forces of utter annihilation insinuated themselves into the ahrimanic policies of the two totalitarian states as Hitler and Stalin shed the blood of their peoples with complete abandon.[24]

One of the ways of keeping Russia from receiving what she needs to receive from Central Europe is the creation of a political or cultural cordon sanitaire between the two, and this is suggested by the 'corridor of intermediaries' which is shown on the 1890 map. To plant a 'diseased seed of the future', it is held necessary by the agents of the Adversary that the spiritual capacities of the Slavic peoples be lamed so that they will not be able to contribute to the sixth epoch what they should. Above all, those agents have considered it necessary that the Slavic peoples be prevented from receiving the highest gifts of the Consciousness Soul Epoch so far: the Rosicrucian impulse in the seventeenth century, the Goethean impulse of the early seventeenth century and anthroposophy in our times.

It was thus to subvert humanity's future that the ahrimanic power groups strove in the 30 years between

1887 and 1917. The next chapter will show how, a hundred years after the Kaiser was 'hypnotized' by *Truth*, another map of the future was published which shows even more clearly that the goals of those power groups have not substantially changed.

2. Here Be Dragons

In Chapter 1 it was argued that a map shown in the British satirical magazine *Truth*, dated Christmas Day 1890 and cited by Arthur Polzer-Hoditz in his book *Kaiser Karl* as an example of the intentions of those who, already before the end of the nineteenth century, were aiming at the creation of a new order in Europe which was to emerge after the anticipated World War, did indeed reveal something of the designs of the western occult brotherhoods whose pre-war maps were referred to by Rudolf Steiner in 1916.[1] Attention was drawn in Chapter 1 to the way in which that 1890 map, presented in such a frivolous and jokey fashion, pointed to disaster especially for Germany and Russia; it indicated that they were to be separated from one another in the post-war order, that Germany would be split up, and Russia would become a 'desert'. In this chapter, two more such maps are brought forward which, it will be argued, similarly reveal something of the political intentions of the western brotherhoods.

The Map of 1888

The first of the two maps was published in the book *Entente Freimauerei und Weltkrieg* (Entente Freemasonry and the World War) by Karl Heise in 1920. The map and Heise's claims are discussed by the historian Renate Riemeck in her book *Mitteleuropa — Bilanz eines Jahrhunderts* (Middle Europe — A Century in the Balance).[2] (The map is reproduced opposite.) Riemeck writes:

> A map, designed in 1888, which in the occult circles of the English-speaking world represented the configuration of Europe as it would be after the World War. There appear to be no indications given for Scandinavia or for a

A map circulating in western brotherhood circles in the 1880s which looked ahead to a newly-shaped Europe after the expected world war; it was published by Karl Heise in his book Entente Freimaurerei und Weltkreig *('Entente Freemasonry and the World War'), Ernst Finkh Verlag, Basel 1920*

particular region of the Latin countries. The map's inscriptions are as follows: 'The area remaining to the Germans (Rhine, Danube)' [A]; 'the Danube-Balkan League which will arise after the prophesied World War (Danube)'[B]; 'the Slav Confederation which will consist of Czechs, Slovaks, Poles, Russians, etc. after the dissolution of the Russian state (Vistula)'.

The small print at the bottom reads: 'Independent from England, but under her influence.'

In her comments on the map, Riemeck writes: 'This goal was only partly realized in the first, but fully accomplished in the second of the (World) Wars of the twentieth century — only the Slav Confederation has not turned out to have quite the form the map's designers intended it would.' Riemeck's book was first published in 1981.[3] She would probably wish to revise that last comment about the Slav Confederation given the developments which have taken place since the attempted coup in Moscow in August 1991 and the subsequent establishment of the Commonwealth of Independent States (CIS)! Alternatively, it could be that the Slav Confederation envisaged by the mapmakers was in fact the system of Soviet control of Eastern Europe from 1945 to 1989, since that included Czechs, Slovaks, and Poles. The 'dissolution of the Russian state' may have referred to the end of czarism, which was a Russian national rather than a Slav institution.

The coastal areas which were to be under English influence might seem to be an anomaly until one realizes that until the Second World War the Eastern Atlantic and the Mediterranean were effectively controlled by the Royal Navy, and after 1945 have been similarly controlled by US armed forces from bases in Iberia, Italy and Greece.

This map, which was presumably intended for 'internal consumption' within the lodges of the western brotherhoods, is said to have originated in 1888, that is, the year after the Prince of Wales and his circle set in motion their diplomatic manoeuvres designed to bring about a British-backed Franco-Russian Alliance which was aimed at Germany and Austria-Hungary.[4] The map which appeared two years later in the satirical magazine *Truth*, and therefore intended for public consumption, is more detailed. But in that map too, it is evident that the main changes affect Germany, Austria-Hungary and Russia. In that 1890 map Finland would have become independent by the end of the coming European war, and Spain and Portugal were to be united, but no radical border changes affected those countries, Italy or Turkey. One gets the impression from both maps that Scandinavia, Britain, France, Iberia, Italy and Turkey were not intended for any really significant change; the focus rather in both maps is on the Germanic and the Slavic countries.

The hidden joke map of 1990

The 'architecture of the new world order' was the subject of an especially thought-provoking article which appeared in *The Economist* magazine on 1 September 1990 at a time when the world's attention was focused in another direction, namely, on the Gulf Crisis. The cover showed a photo of an Arab prince with a falcon on his wrist and the issue's cover title was 'The old order passes'. It seemed to refer to the end of autocracy in the Middle East as a consequence of the Gulf crisis, but up in the corner where other articles were listed was a reference to an innocuous-sounding article titled 'A New Flag: A survey of defence and the democracies' (see illustrations, p.54). This article turned out to be in fact the main feature of the magazine that week. The 'new' flag referred to was actually the Stars and Stripes, a large photo of which introduced the article. But the stars were not arranged in their usual rows. They had become the circlet of stars of the European Community. It was as if the EC had

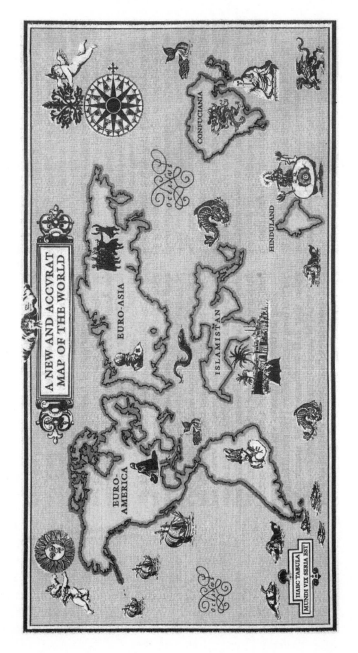

become part of the USA, and reading between the lines it is clear that this is more or less what the author had in mind. A fully-fledged standing alliance between Europe and America is proposed which would take over from NATO. This alliance would lead to ever-closer economic and cultural ties across the Atlantic.

The author goes on to illustrate a new ideas-based world with a map — the third in our trio — 'a new and accvrat [sic] map of the world', illustrated in a jokey mock-Renaissance style complete with cherubs, sea monsters and a Latin inscription (see illustration p.54). The author intends that this shall replace the previous ideas-based map of the world, namely, that of the capitalist-Communist blocs. He rearranges the geography of the world to fit his new culture-based ideology. Europe is joined to North and South America. A stretch of water divides this Euro-America from Euro-Asia. Eastern Europe, including Greece, the Balkans and Romania, is split off from the rest of Europe and belongs to Euro-Asia. To the south, separated by a larger body of water meant to symbolize ideological and psychological 'distance', is the Muslim world of 'Islamistan' — North Africa, Turkey, the Middle East, Iran, Afghanistan, Pakistan and Indonesia. The fact that it includes Turkey is of interest, given Turkey's present efforts to join the European Community. An even larger body of water separates the two continents of 'Hinduland' (India) and Confuciania (the Far East plus Indo-China) from each other and from the other continents. Africa below the Sahara and Australasia seem to have disappeared from the author's world altogether.

Interestingly enough, the map shows the sun over the western hemisphere, rather than over Asia, where, traditionally, one might expect to find it. Each continent is given a symbol. That of Euro-America is a seventeenth-century Puritan whose prayerful gaze seems to be directed to the conveniently placed sun. The European half of Euro-

America is not deemed worthy of its own symbol; the Puritan is obviously intended to symbolize the transition from Europe to America. Latin America, although part of Euro-America, by contrast does have its own symbol, which would appear to be one of the *conquistadors*; in other words, in both north and south, a connection is made between America and the Western European countries. The symbol of the Islamic world is three men, their backs to the reader, huddled outside a town, perhaps in prayer, perhaps plotting a murder or discussing a camel sale. One sees the three men, a town, some trees; one does not see one person, as is the case in Euro-America and Euro-Asia, and, as one might expect, no representation of spiritual beings such as are seen in Hinduland and Confuciania. The symbol for Euro-Asia looks like a Patriarch of the Russian Orthodox Church, who is shown looking to the south-east rather than to the west. Over in Siberia are some six men, two of whom are dancing figures who bear a certain resemblance to Cossacks. Dancing is normally associated with the feet, which in traditional astrological terms are ruled by the sign of Pisces, and Pisces is the astrological sign normally identified with Russia on account of its position as the last zodiac sign, the 'latecomer', the cosmic dreamer, the nebulous one with an infinite capacity for feeling and suffering. This is not to say that this is why the dancers were chosen to represent Euro-Asia (i.e. Russia); the mapmakers may merely have wished to fill in space and chosen an image of Russia which they imagined would be readily recognizable. Nevertheless, the nature, positions, and associations of the symbols ought to be considered.

For some unexplained reason, Hinduland (India) is shown very small. Its symbol is a Hindu god standing behind what looks like a cosmic egg in which is shown a wheel. Flanking the god and connected to him by a stream emerging from his mouth are two beings; the one on his left has a tail, wings and two horns, while the one on his right appears somewhat more delicate and 'angelic'. Crouching above the wheel (of life?) are two tiny human figures. What we see here then is a symbol stressing a spiritual, mythological aspect. The symbols of Confuciania are a Chinese dragon and a Buddhist monk sitting in meditation, holding a string of prayer beads and what may be a *vajra* thunderbolt symbol. It is possible that the monk is meant to be associated with Japan.

To summarize:

Euro-America: a single kneeling Puritan and a military *conquistador*

Europe proper — no symbol

Euro-Asia: a single Orthodox Patriarch, representative of a hierarchical religious order, and a group of dancing Cossacks

Islamistan: three huddled men, trees and a town, minarets

Hinduland: a mythological and seemingly dualistic representation of the beings behind the cosmic order

Confuciania: a mythological dragon and a meditating monk

Clearly, the symbols were chosen with some thought. What of the map's other features?

In the world's oceans we see various monsters, fish, a sea serpent and a griffin, twelve in all. The griffin would appear to be out of place, not being a sea creature. There are also three human creations, namely, ships, and these are all sailing towards the west coast of Euro-America. There are three aerial or heavenly beings, cherubs, one holding the sun over America, one holding a compass, east of Euro-Asia, and one blowing wind above the map's title. To the left of his head is some handwriting so miniscule it is difficult to make out. Lastly, in the bottom left-hand corner is a box in which is written the Latin phrase *HAEC TABULA MUNDI VIX SERIA EST* (This map of the world is hardly serious)!

But we can be sure that it is very serious. Otherwise the author would not have gone to the trouble of devising or comissioning it and including it in his article, which although written in the usual rather flippant style of *The Economist* is only too serious in its import. As was the case with the 1890 map in *Truth* magazine, also intended for public consumption, the author's spoof on a Renaissance map is presented in a jokey manner.

A map of ideologies

The Economist author considers it 'a useful mental exercise to redraw the map of the world so that it shows bodies of ideas, not lumps of land. On this new map North America and the western part of Europe—up to and including the Finns, the Balts, the Poles, the Hungarians, and the northern part of Yugoslavia—are a single continent.' (Note the veiled reference to Croatia and Slovenia.) After describing the map's other features, he says:

> This is a decorative way of saying that America and part of Europe have something big in common that they share with nobody else, not even the other part of what used to be called Christendom. They are the children of the RRE, the Renaissance, the Reformation and the Enlightenment: those three interconnected upheavals ... that created the modern world. The RRE was a flowering of individual consciousness ... It took its purest form in Protestantism [hence the Puritan facing the sun], though it is now accepted in most of the Catholic world; but those three great upheavals all took place outside the Orthodox zone of Christianity.

At first glance, this might seem reasonable, but let us look a little closer at what he is doing here. First, it is clear that he is really only interested in the Europe-America relationship. His map of the world is designed primarily to underpin that, which is understandable, since his article focuses on the need for a standing alliance between the two. India, Africa, Australasia and the Far East figure not at all in its 16 pages. While those familiar with Rudolf Steiner's work will recognize in the author's 'flowering of the individual consciousness' the hallmark of the Epoch of the Consciousness Soul, which began with the Renaissance, the author's historical reasoning ought to be questioned. It cannot be said that the Reformation was any more 'interconnected' with the Enlightenment than the Middle Ages were 'interconnected' with the Renaissance or the Reformation. The Renaissance and the Reformation did not emerge from nowhere. During the period of the High Middle Ages (*c.* 1150–1500) it is clearly discernible how the culture of medieval Catholic Christendom with its authoritarian attitudes and modes of behaviour was in the process of breaking down and how the new era of Renaissance humanism and free spiritual enquiry, beginning in Italy (in Pico della Mirandola, Leonardo da Vinci, *et al.*), was emerging out of it.

Secondly, a wedge has been driven by the map separating the Christians of Eastern and Western Europe. The implication is that it is not Christianity that is so important but rather the individualism of the RRE with its tendency toward secular humanism. The author maintains that this (highly questionable) view of history 'proves' the need for a new special relationship across the Atlantic in that Russia could not be part of Euro-America because it had not shared in the RRE. The new alliance, it is argued, must be based on shared ideas and values.

Europe and the US – 1984 revisited

After the events of 1989, the US and British media were full of statements by politicians, military figures, and media commentators that an American military presence must

remain in Europe to 'help maintain stability'. These statements are invariably vague. For example, Henry Kissinger,
writing in *The Washington Post*: 'NATO is needed because it
remains the sole institutional link between America and
Europe ... What is needed between the United States and
Western Europe is not more structure but something
intangible like the special relationship that has always
existed between America and Britain.'[5] In a similar vein,
former Prime Minister of Japan, Yasuhiro Nakasone,
speaking at a reception (10 April 1992) for a Japanese and
American Leadership Conference held in Kyoto said that 'a
new, wider role for the Japanese-American Security Treaty
(a Far Eastern equivalent of NATO) must be created; it must
become more political and cultural. We have to start now to
see that people understand this.' In his article, Kissinger
also wrote: 'The European Community should encourage a
larger political role for the United States within its delib-
erations ... France must not stand in the way of a larger
American role in political consultations.' It might seem as
though Kissinger wants a more intangible relationship in
contrast to the 'standing alliance' advocated in the article.
But in fact Kissinger is all in favour of a strengthened
though more flexible NATO which will bind America and
Europe even closer together.

The Economist author, for his part, writes: 'On the
European side it will be necessary to accept that the new
entity Europe is trying to create ... will be part of another,
wider, looser entity that includes North America.'
Europeans and Americans, he says, 'should both at long last
recognize that they are part of each other, as of nowhere
else, in a permanent way'. Differences can often be found
between those, like Kissinger and the author of the 1990
Economist article, who argue for a closer relationship
between Europe and America. But in essence their stance is
the same: the two should become one; Europe should
follow the American (or white Anglo-Saxon Protestant)

way — the European Community flag must become part of the American flag. Similarly, Margaret Thatcher clearly felt and stated on many occasions that 'the Europeans' ought to follow Britain's (i.e. the Anglo-Saxon) lead. Their 'ideals' and 'philosophies', she maintained, are simply not grounded in reality as is the 'common-sense, pragmatic' approach of the British![6]

However, it is not just on the basis of a cosy cultural affinity between America and Western Europe that a 'permanent standing alliance' was advocated in the article. In the New World Order of the twenty-first century, he sees three main threats facing 'Euro-America' which will replace Soviet Communism. These are: the new Russia (again), the Muslim world (fundamentalism and immigration) and Germany (resurgent nationalism). From the US standpoint, these three 'threats' all stem from the 'East'. Interestingly enough, 'Confuciania' does not figure among these threats, despite American media hype in the 80s and 90s about Japan and China respectively replacing the USSR as the chief threat to America's way of life. *The Economist* author urges that the three threats need, in effect, a new 'containment', hence the need for a standing alliance.

What we see in his map is similar to the world of George Orwell's *Nineteen Eighty-Four* nightmare: Euro-America (Oceania, the Anglo-Saxon dominated world), Euro-Asia (Eurasia, the Slav-dominated world), and Confuciania (Eastasia, the Mongoloid dominated world). These are to be the Great Powers of the twenty-first century, and Islamistan, Hinduland and Africa are no doubt intended as the battlegrounds between them. In 1984 numerous media pundits assured us that Orwell's vision had no relevance whatsoever to the then current situation.

Could it be that these three threats are posited because Germany, Russia and Islam represent major spiritual challenges to what Rudolf Steiner called 'Americanism' (American commercial materialism), which is the main vehicle for Ahriman's approaching incarnation.[7] Unlike some in the US media, *The Economist* author does not regard Japan as a threat, because he follows the long-held policy of *The Economist*, which since the late 1950s has been very pro-Japanese; *The Economist* view is that Japan can be kept safely tucked under America's wing. Its energies can therefore be used for Americanism's (read 'Ahriman's) benefit. The 1990 article does not mention another spiritual challenge to the materialist culture of America — that of the Vatican. It is not 'the done thing' any more to speak openly of the Vatican as an enemy of the Protestant West. If the challenges from Islam, from Rome, and from the Far East can in a sense all be seen as 'luciferic challenges' stemming from the past (the fourth and third post-Atlantean epochs), the challenges from Germany and Russia are those of the present and the future respectively (the fifth and sixth epochs), and are therefore ultimately more dangerous to Ahriman.

Russia and the Slavic world

The article describes Russia in condescending terms: it 'is trying hard to be a nicer place than it has ever been before, but [it] is still Russia ... Assume the total disintegration of the Soviet Union, meaning that the Russian Republic is abandoned by all the other 14 Soviet Republics, even its fellow Slavs in the Ukraine and Belorussia.' This article appeared in September 1990, before most people in the West could even conceive of an independent Belorussia, now known as Belarus. The author goes on to conjure up a fearful picture of Russia in the year 2000, still with a huge population, a massive armoury, and an improved economy, and then says: 'On the whole this Russia will be an easier place to live with than it has been for the past 70 years. Yet, on any assumption except a highly implausible one, its sheer size will make its European neighbours want to keep a wary eye on it. The *only* [emphasis added] assumption on which it would be safe to say there was no longer any need to worry about Russia is (a) that Russia becomes a full democracy in the sense in which other Europeans use that word and (b) that full democracies never fight with each other.' He goes on to argue that these two assumptions do not hold and that democracy functions best when people are able to confront authority. 'The Russians,' he says, 'are not yet that sort of people. It is not their fault. Their history has been overloaded with authority, and they never had the great authority-eroding experience of Western Europe's sixteenth and seventeenth centuries.' (What about traditionally authoritarian Japan, one wonders, which *The Economist* never tires of repeating shares 'common democratic and economic values' with the West.) This is the same obsessive view of Russia, only presented in a less aggressive fashion, as was propagated by the father of America's post-war containment policy, George Kennan. He believed that it was not the Soviets that were the real enemy of the West, but Russia itself, owing to its historical and cultural traditions, and that the West could protect itself only by a western policy of *realpolitik* that granted Russia its own sphere of influence, or zone of quarantine, and 'contained' it within that.[8]

The same view of a non-Communist Russia as a potential threat to the West was constantly reiterated by high-profile Anglo-American observers such as Henry Kissinger, Richard Nixon, Caspar Weinberger, Michael Heseltine and others.[9] These people have harped on the danger of nuclear weapons in the hands of a new nationalistic Russian authoritarianism, but beneath their dire warnings one can detect deeper, more spiritually-oriented motivations such as those hinted at by writers like Francis Fukuyama and the author of the 1990 *Economist* article, themselves in close contact with Anglo-American circles of power. The occult background to those motivations was discussed in greater detail at the end of Chapter 1 of this book. To recall, it is to

block the proper spiritual impulse of the sixth post-
Atlantean epoch (AD 3573–5733), that of true spiritualized
community, the introducing of which will be the particular
responsibility of the Slavic peoples. Blocking this can be
done by flooding Slavic culture with materialism and by
preventing the Slavs from forming a right connection with
the legitimate spiritual impulses of the present fifth epoch,
which are Rosicrucian, Goetheanistic, anthroposophical.
The bridge from the fifth to the sixth epochs would thereby
be removed. It is for this reason that, for all his emphasis on
the heritage of the French Revolution and the eighteenth-
century Enlightenment, Francis Fukuyama not once in his
339-page book[10] uses the word 'fraternity', not even in the
index; and in the speeches of Margaret Thatcher, fraternity
never figured alongside liberty and equality. The concept of
a spiritual brotherhood, a community of the spirit, is one
which the western 'brotherhoods' wish to keep to themselves, although in their hierarchical brotherhoods there is
neither liberty of self-expression nor equality.[11]

Breaking the link between Central and Eastern Europe

The political goals of the ahrimanic forces are to separate
Russia from the rest of Europe, and particularly from
Germanic culture where the Rosicrucian, Goetheanistic,
and anthroposophical impulses originated, so that a direct
connection can be made between the West and the East,
omitting Central Europe, just as such a direct connection
existed during the Cold War despite a superficial political
antagonism. In fact, the destiny of Russia has been grossly
interfered with and largely determined by western occult
circles since at least the creation of the Franco-Russian
Alliance in 1894.[12]
   That the isolation of Russia is intended also to be physical
is evident from the 'narrow but frequently turbulent stretch
of water' by which the article writer separates Russia from

the rest of Europe. As Prime Minister, Margaret Thatcher always spoke about the three great European cities of Prague, Budapest and Warsaw, and how important it was that Czechoslovakia, Hungary and Poland should be welcomed into the fold by Western Europe as soon as possible. She never had anything to say about Belgrade, Sofia or Bucharest. Similarly, Henry Kissinger:

> *No issue is more urgent* [emphasis added] than to relate the former Soviet satellites of Eastern Europe to Western Europe and NATO. At least Poland, Czechoslovakia and Hungary should be permitted to join the Community rapidly ... Morover, if a no-man's land is to be avoided in Eastern Europe, NATO ought to leave no doubt that pressures against these countries would be treated as a challenge to western security, whatever the formal aspect of this undertaking.[13]

Kissinger did not say why 'no issue is more important', although in his extensive article on the Atlantic Alliance covering virtually a whole page of a newspaper this issue was discussed in only two short paragraphs!

It might be objected that, since the Poles, Czechs and Hungarians are Slavs too and thus also surely people of the sixth epoch, why aren't the western brotherhoods also seeking to quarantine them. The answer lies in Russia's unique geography and history, for she is the only European nation that has had extensive centuries-long experience of dealing with the Mongoloid peoples of the Far East — Tartars, Chinese and Japanese. Russia acts as a bridge between Europe and East Asia in the same way as Germany does between Western and Eastern Europe. This experience the Western Slavs do not possess; they themselves are the bridgeway between Central Europe and Russia, a bridgeway which the Anglo-American power circles are seeking to cut by luring them into the American-dominated structures of the EU and NATO.[14] In July 1997 Poland, the Czech

Young academics Kissinger and Brzezinski in 1965 at the Council on Foreign Relations in New York

Francis Fukuyama, former deputy director of the US State Department's Policy Planning Staff, and RAND Corporation consultant. Currently (2013) Senior Fellow at Stanford University

Republic and Hungary joined NATO as has been the intention of the western brotherhoods for the last five years at least, and their plans have taken another significant step forward.

Some Russians are evidently awake to the attempt to cut them off from the rest of Europe. *Le Monde* reported fears in Moscow that the Ukrainians were planning the formation of 'an axis stretching from the Black Sea to the Baltic and taking in Belarus and vast territories once forming the Grand Duchy of Lithuania. Moscow's daily *Independent* fantasized freely on the subject in an astonishing front-page speculation about the possible creation of a "cordon sanitaire" between Russia and Europe.'[15] Maybe they had been reading *The Economist*, not normally regarded as a magazine given to fantasy! Or they may have heard Lord Carrington speaking on BBC Radio's *World At One* news programme in June 1990. Speaking about the need for the West to modernize its defences despite the events of 1989, he mentioned almost in passing that the possibility of setting up some kind of cordon sanitaire between the Soviet Union and Western Europe should be investigated. On the *PM* news programme later that same day, his 'aside' had become a 20-minute feature, and in a BBC TV interview the following month, the Foreign Secretary Douglas Hurd revealed that the creation of a zone of neutral countries from the Baltic to the Black Sea was an idea that the government was 'looking at'.[16] Carrington would thus seem to have been advocating a 'no-man's land' while Kissinger was against the idea, but one should recall the words of Rudolf Steiner:

> Do not believe that there can be no individuals who are not Jesuit *and* Freemason. They have progressed beyond the point of working in one direction only. They know that it is necessary to tackle situations from various sides in order to push matters in a particular direction ... it is a matter of exercising influence by means of suggestion.

You can do one thing and say another, you can say something different from what you are doing, and you can often do something that seems to be the opposite of what is supposed to happen and what you are really doing.[17]

This is the way these circles work. It is not to suggest that Carrington and Kissinger are Jesuit or Freemason, but that two such close associates as these may deliberately put forward seemingly opposing or contradictory solutions in the service of the same ultimate common goal.

Again and again representatives of the Anglo-American viewpoint, such as Kissinger and *The Economist*, stress the danger of a close liaison between Germany and Russia. Kissinger: 'It is in nobody's interest for Germany and Russia to perceive each other as their principal policy options. If they become too close, they raise the danger of hegemony; if they quarrel, they will involve the world in escalating crisis.' 'Without America, Britain and France cannot sustain the political balance in Western Europe; Germany would lack an anchor to check nationalistic ambitions and outside pressures; Russia would not have a long-term partner in global affairs.' (Note the vagueness of that last phrase; it was not clarified in the rest of the article.) 'A challenge [to US security and economy] could evolve from chaos on the territory of the former Soviet Union, from ethnic conflicts and political instability in Eastern Europe, and from the redefinition of Germany's role.'[18] *The Economist* article cleverly puts the point across through the use of pictures and captions. There is a picture of Shevardnadze, then Soviet Foreign Minister, walking with Germany's Genscher on his right and James Baker on his left; the caption underneath reads: 'The right three, the wrong way round.' Another photograph shows Kohl and Gorbachev chatting at their July 1990 Stavropol meeting; the caption reads: 'Good for Germany and Russia to see eye to eye—but not alone'. In other words, Uncle Sam must always be there too between them. There is not the space here to present the various other subtle ways in which the message is insinuated that not only are Germany and Russia to be considered like two ex-rapists who, having served time, are now out on parole, but they must be watched very warily in case they relapse; these two former criminals must also on no account be allowed to get to know each other too well.

In the conclusion to the article we read:

> Perhaps history got its timing wrong. If the collapse of European Communism (which was the necessary condition of the reuniting of Germany) had happened a generation later, the countries of democratic Europe might by then have been cohesive enough to cope with the consequences. The nervousness about German power would have been less, since 'Germany' would have meant something different in a more woven-together Europe. This new Europe would have been more capable of organizing a single army and a single nuclear force. It might, in short, have been able to do without America: which would have been a pity for many other reasons, but might have been at least militarily feasible. But history was impatient, and the change happened before those things came about.

The implication here that 'history' was moving in its own mysterious way which nobody can understand or anticipate is an idea that has been voiced in the media countless times since the upheavals of 1989. As Disraeli said through the mouth of one of his characters in his political novel *Coningsby* (written in 1843): 'the world is governed by very different personages from what is imagined by those who are not behind the scenes' and those 'different personages' understand only too well, as Rudolf Steiner indicated many times, what the laws of history (i.e. human development) are and how they can be used to suit their own self-interest.

The new *Pax Romana*

In 1992 the *New York Times* managed to obtain a classified US Defense Department memorandum, which described itself as 'definitive guidance from the Secretary of Defense' intended to help 'set the nation's direction for the next century'.[19] It spoke of a strategy

> to 'establish and protect a new order' that accounts 'sufficiently for the interests of the advanced industrial nations to discourage them from challenging our leadership', while at the same time maintaining a military dominance capable of 'deterring potential competitors from even aspiring to a larger regional or global role' ... the document argues not only for preserving but expanding the most demanding American commitments and for resisting efforts by key allies to provide for their own security... 'we will retain the pre-eminent responsibility for addressing selectively those wrongs which threaten not only our interests, but those of our allies or friends, or which could seriously unsettle international relations' ... Much of the document parallels the extensive public statements of Defense Secretary Richard B. Cheney and Gen. Colin L. Powell, chairman of the Joint Chiefs of Staff ... The new memo gives central billing to US efforts to prevent emergence of a rival superpower... 'to prevent any hostile power from dominating a region whose resources would ... be sufficient to generate global power. These regions include Western Europe, East Asia, the territory of the former Soviet Union, and Southwest Asia.'

In other words, Confuciania, Euro-Asia, and Islamistan.

The imperial ambitions of this memorandum speak for themselves; only the *form* of the imperium has changed. In 1992, when those words were written, the world was 579 years into the fifth post-Atlantean epoch which, according to Rudolf Steiner, began in 1413. Five hundred and seventy-nine years from the beginning of the fourth post-Atlantean epoch, which began in 747 BC, takes us to 168 BC. In that year Rome defeated Macedonia at the Battle of Pydna; it was a defeat which signified the final disintegration of the empire of Alexander the Great. In 146 BC, Rome destroyed Carthage and Corinth. The path from Italian republic to world empire was clear.

Europe in a threefold world

From the end of the 1980s there was ever more talk in the media of three economic regions, centring on the three great money blocs of the dollar, the Deutschmark and the yen. The end of the Cold War, it seemed, was coinciding with the end of the post-war economic dispensation, which was largely an American creation. Protectionism was replacing free trade; we were told: 'free trade has enriched the world for the last 40 years just as the nuclear balance of terror has brought peace to the world' — although what the poverty-stricken masses of the Third World, and the peoples of Cambodia, Vietnam, Afghanistan, Angola and a dozen other countries would make of such claims is another matter. Essentially, when talking about the world's 'peace' and 'wealth', English-speaking media commentators invariably have in mind the white (especially the Anglo-Saxon) peoples and nations.

At the end of the First World War, Rudolf Steiner brought forward the imagination of the Threefold Social Order as a spiritual-cultural response of Central Europe both to the abstract illusory Fourteen Points of President Woodrow Wilson of America and to the statist programmes of the Russian Bolsheviks Lenin and Trotsky. These schemes from America and Russia were strongly criticized by Rudolf Steiner for their utter illusionism, and the subsequent history of the twentieth century has more than borne him out.

By the Threefold Social Order, Steiner pointed to an impulse that he believed to be actually moving within the subconscious wills of modern humanity in the fifth post-Atlantean epoch. It was an impulse that was seeking to be realized and which *would* be realized, even if in distorted form, because it corresponds to the deepest needs of humanity in our epoch. In essence, it means that whereas the political sphere of law and rights had in the medieval period largely emancipated itself from the spiritual or religious sphere, in our epoch, since the fifteenth century, the economic sphere has been seeking to emancipate itself from the political state. The three main realms of social life—the spiritual-cultural, the political-legal and the economic—need to be independent and have their own manner of working, while yet remaining in relationship with each other. All too many of the problems of modern society stem from the fact that we have not properly separated out the three spheres from each other. There is still interference in the one sphere from the other two. This separation of the spheres has to do with the differing tasks of the three post-Atlantean cultural epochs. The third epoch (2907–747 BC) was the age when human beings developed their feeling life, when all social life was subject to divine commands and to the spiritual dimension. The fourth epoch (747 BC—AD 1413) was the age when humanity learned to think for itself and apply its thought processes to its social arrangements instead of receiving them as divine revelations. And the fifth epoch (AD 1413–3573), of which not even a third has yet been completed, is one in which human thinking must fully penetrate the physical sense world and in which humanity must develop a self-realized morality commensurate with human freedom—man's independent thinking dedicated to doing the good rather than merely satisfying selfish personal desires.

The third epoch was pre-eminently that of religion, of the spirit, of man's relationship to God. The fourth was that of society, in which people worked out new forms of social relationships, new social ideas on the basis of their thinking about social relationships. It was the time in which, for example, the Greeks developed the civic ideas of the *polis*, and the Romans the idea of the citizen. Religion of course continued to be a major factor, but we are here considering what was a new development in evolution. In the fifth epoch, we are faced with the task of setting in order our relationship with the world of nature itself, with the earth and the bounty it makes available to us for produce and manufacture to satisfy our common needs. In the eighteenth century, there seemed to have emerged out of the European collective consciousness—though according to Rudolf Steiner it was actually the inspiration of Rosicrucian initiates—a motto which encapsulated in three words this entire development of five thousand years: Liberty, Equality, Fraternity. These three words expressed in the more abstract language of the fifth epoch what Christ had expressed 1800 years before when He said: I am the Way (Fraternity), the Truth (Liberty), and the Life (Equality).

Rudolf Steiner showed how liberty (human freedom) needs to be paramount in the spiritual-cultural sphere, where our individuality is to be respected; equality should be paramount in the political-legal sphere where we all have rights and responsibilities as equal members of the community; and fraternity (mutual service) ought to be the key principle of the economic life. The modern division of labour illustrates this well: without each other's help, we cannot transform the gifts of nature into useful products for each other. These three spheres are to be separately membered and organized and interrelating links between them created.

Anthroposophy, the wisdom of man, implies that the human being is a microcosm of the universe—all levels of reality are to be found within the human spiritual-physical organism. During the First World War Steiner developed his insights into the threefold nature of the human physical organism: the nerve-sense system, the rhythmic system, and the metabolic-limb system. He also showed how the human being's higher faculties were related to these three physical systems and, furthermore, how the whole of humanity could be described as a single being extending over the globe. Asia represents the geographic 'head' of humanity, Europe and Africa are the 'rhythmic-heart' system of the world, while the American continent is the world's metabolic-limb system. The reality of this spatial configuration is echoed in human history in that the head, Asia, is where human civilization in the post-Atlantean epochs really began. Civilization then proceeded steadily westwards, Europe becoming the focus of new social developments in the fourth and early fifth epochs; and America has become the focus now as we go deeper into modern industrial and post-industrial civilization.

These three broad cultural regions, America, Europe-Africa and Asia, have now become separate. America having developed out of Europe, and with much of European civilization, including Christianity, having grown out of Asia, the three are seeking to relate to each other—but in a way that is appropriate for the fifth epoch, which is led by economics, as the fourth was by the state, and the third by religion. This is also a reflection of what Steiner meant by the threefolding impulse working within the unconscious will of humanity in our time. The adversary forces have to work with this development and will try to turn it to their advantage. Their aims in this direction will be further discussed in detail in Chapter 3, but in general it can be said here that they will seek to confuse our understanding of the three spheres and blur the demarcation between them (by mixing the political with the economic, for example).

If, then, the three regional economic blocs were to

develop new forms of 'continental' nationalism, or 'continentalism', another form of 'us' against 'them', it could turn out that large areas of what used to be called the Third World would become the economic or even proxy military battleground of the three world powers. The English-speaking world's élite has already made a new bid for control in Africa, as the cataclysmic events in Rwanda since 1994 and in Zaire/Congo in 1996–97 have shown. The scenario of inter-continental conflict was that of Orwell's *Nineteen Eighty-Four*; it was taken to an extreme in the depiction of the mass hate sessions depicted in that book. Such a conflict would be disastrous, and no doubt the ahrimanic and luciferic powers will strive to bring it about. But assuming the three economic blocs are as successful as the adversaries in the Cold War in preventing any nuclear conflict between them, even if they turn out to be rivals, a world of three huge economic confederations in which individual nations retain cultural and political — as distinct from economic — autonomy may still be a step forward.

A configuration of the world into three trading blocs, three 'Single Markets', is then not necessarily a negative development, in that it may well serve to bring together diverse peoples and nations, fostering cosmopolitanism and thus ending the often ruinous preoccupations of the nation state in so far as nationalism in economics has had a disastrous effect on international relations. Such cosmopolitanism in the economic arena could have a very positive dimension, leading us further along the path to a consciousness of sharing the resources of the world and of economic interdependence. This would contribute to the development of a spirit of fraternity in the economic realm. Hopefully, this stage of three economic blocs and their interrelationships would lead on to a genuine Single World Economy, which would be based on the recognition that in the world economy there is a true division of labour which makes us all dependent on each other and jointly responsible for our management and exploitation of the world's resources.

At a point during the Koberwitz course of lectures given in the summer of 1924, Rudolf Steiner apparently said that there would be a United States of Europe analogous to the United States of America. To the question when this would occur, he replied: in about 70 years' time (1992? 1994?). As long as the peoples of Europe avoid the possible downsides to this — excessive bureaucratic centralism, 'possession' by the ghost of the Roman Empire, and the homogenizing cultural uniformity of Americanism — a supranational economic union, a European Confederal Union, which came together because the people (not just the mandarins) willed it to, could play a significant role in promoting a harmony among peoples of different backgrounds. The Folk Spirits ('Guardian Archangels') of various tribes joined forces in the Middle Ages creating vessels into which could incarnate new mightier Spirits who then became the Folk Spirits of the new nation states. Is a similar process now underway under the leadership of Michael, the ruling Time Spirit of this part (1879–2233) of the fifth epoch? This will not mean the end of national Folk Spirits, because these are closely bound up with the national languages of Europe, which are not about to disappear. Instead, under Michael's leadership, it is to be hoped that the Folk Spirits will come together in a spirit of cooperation, which will enable human beings to develop cross-border economic communities fostering fraternity.

Is it because many people in Britain are unable to recognize the inexorability of any such process of historical development that they strenuously oppose the EU and all its works? The reference here is not to those who wish to reform the EU or who wish to make it more efficient, but to those whose visceral reactions to it are rooted in the superiority complexes of the past age of nation states, the era of Gabriel (1525–1879). How many Britons recognize that after its period of continental engagement in the Middle Ages, marked by the Norman Conquest of 1066 and the defeat of the English by Joan of Arc in 1429, Britain under the Tudors entered a period of psychological 'insularity' so that it could find itself before embarking on its new world role after 1600? How many see that today Britain may need to 'return' to the continent which made it, in order to play its part in helping to forge a new identity for Europe in the emerging threefold world community?

A lack of historical imagination and insight would prevent the British from seeing the stages of development they have passed through to get to where they are now; it would block understanding of where they need to go next. In the same way, the English may fail to recognize that the Scots and the Welsh are clamouring for separation, not as the result of a backward-looking narrow nationalism but because the task they had to perform together with the English, namely, the creation and administration of the world-spanning British Empire, is over, and they wish to return to their former status as independent European peoples. The English needed the help of the three Celtic peoples of the British Isles in order to take on their world role, and indeed, the enormous part played by the Celtic peoples in the enterprise of Empire is well-documented. To seek to preserve the Union just because we are familiar with it or because of some vague unsubstantiated fears that we will all be worse off without it is short-sighted in the extreme. Unfortunately, the 250 years at the top, so to speak, have had such a profound effect on the English that it is difficult for them to relinquish their attachment to the historical realities of the age of Gabriel. Despite having given up most of their navy, for example, since 1945, both Royal and Merchant, all too many of them still see themselves as having a world role, even if only vicariously through the military, cultural and economic reach of the United States. They still wish to indulge in the old illusion of Britain 'punching above its weight'. Actually, Britain always did this, even at the height of Empire; the whole imperial show was largely a supreme confidence trick. It had to be, when only 5000 civil servants supervised hundreds of millions of overseas subjects.

Britain — or rather, England — then needs to recognize its new humbler status and role in 'returning' to Europe, helping to forge Europe's economic union and, putting 300 years of experience to use, helping to facilitate the European Economic Union's relations with the wider world. On the other hand, the opposition of many other, more perceptive Britons to the EU project is based on a healthy instinctive recognition that a United States of Europe on the American federal model, a political superstate, is being stealthily constructed by groups of unknown bureaucrats in a manner which can hardly be called democratic.

Since the Second World War, this project has been pushed forward both by continental Roman Catholic thinkers and political activists, and also by the American East Coast Establishment. Playing a key part in connecting the two groups, the continental and the American, were shadowy string-pullers such as Jean Monnet and Joseph Retinger[20] who worked with consummate effectiveness behind the scenes, avoiding the glare of publicity. Behind the Catholic drive to a united Europe lies the old dream of a resurrected medieval Holy Roman Empire under the spiritual leadership of the Papacy — the old ghost of the *imperium Romanum*. Since the Papacy first hitched its star to the Merovingian monarchy of the Franks under Clovis I, the French state has all too often been the Papacy's prime political instrument. Robert Schuman, the French Foreign Minister who gave his name to the Plan which established the original forerunner of the EU, the European Coal and Steel Community in 1950, was a lifelong Catholic activist. Schuman hailed from Alsace, the age-old bone of contention between France and Germany, and he forged a

Churchill and Retinger at the Congress of the Hague May 1948.
Retinger is seated behind Churchill, with his chin on his fist

The New Lotharingians, Robert Schuman and Jean Monnet

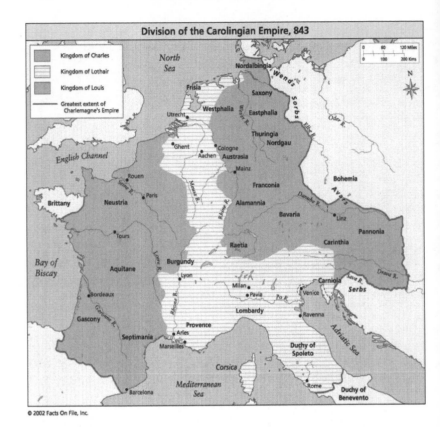

Division of the Carolingian Empire, 843

The divisions of Charlemagne's Empire after the Treaty of Verdun in 843. Note the central state of Lotharingia (Lorraine)

close working relationship with another strong Catholic politician, Konrad Adenauer, the first post-war German Chancellor, who was a Rhinelander. Much in the thoughts of these two men in the late 40s and early 50s was the reconstruction of a kind of latter-day Lotharingia (Lorraine) between France and Germany. This was the old Carolingian state which had been born when Charlemagne's three

grandsons divided his Empire between them at the parti-
tion of Verdun in 843. It ran from Holland in the north,
through modern Belgium, and included much of the Rhi-
neland area, Switzerland, Burgundy, Savoy and northern
Italy. Its life was short, and it was effectively terminated
after only 26 years, in 869 when Charles the Bald of France
marched his army into Lotharingia. The following year,
Lotharingia was divided between the two surviving
brothers, Charles of France and Ludwig the German. Its
Italian rump went on to become a nascent Italy. In that
period 843–70, the ancestors of three great European cultures were born.

The significance of the year 869

Rudolf Steiner indicated that there are certain key years in
history which function as axial points. Relationships can be
seen in the years which lie on either side of them. Thus, with
1879 as axis, the spiritual events of the year 1878 are
reflected in the earthly events of 1880. The year 1413, the
beginning of the fifth post-Atlantean epoch, was another
such year. From 1413 to 1957 = 544 years, and 1413 – 544 =
869. The year 1957 was that of the signing of the Treaty of
Rome which established the EEC. It was built above all on,
and has since revolved around, the relationship between
France and Germany and, in the late 1950s and early 1960s,
depended very much on the personal relationship between
Adenauer and Charles De Gaulle (Charles of France), both
men who regarded the empire of Charlemagne with some
nostalgia and frequently alluded to it. Charlemagne, of
course, had been crowned Holy Roman Emperor by Pope
Leo III in 800 in Rome. Around the axial point of 1413, 800
corresponds to the year 2026, while Charlemagne's accession as King of the Franks in 771 corresponds to 2055. The
Carolingian Empire came to an end with the deposition of

Charles the Fat in 887, which corresponds to 1939. From 1939 till either 2026 or 2055 is that period in the modern age which resonates with the events of the Carolingian Empire. We can ask: is it an accident that the European Union, built on the Franco-German axis, is emerging in precisely this period which corresponds to the life of the Carolingian Empire? And who are the individuals who are playing the key roles in this process?

The year 869 is also significant because Rudolf Steiner often drew attention to the eighth Ecumenical Council of Constantinople which took place in the church of the Hagia Sophia (the Holy Spirit) and where the Papal delegates managed to force the rest of the Church to anathematize the doctrine of the 'twin souls' which the Patriarch Photius of Constantinople had been teaching. By one of these 'twin souls' Photius meant the immortal human spirit. The 11th canon of the Council denied the existence of such a 'twin soul', declared that there was only one soul, which had some vaguely stated 'spiritual attributes', and thus effectively reduced the human being from a threefold entelechy (body, soul and spirit) to a twofold one (body and soul, or mind and body). This concept of the human being as a twofold being remains the norm in the West to this day. By denying the existence of the spirit, the western Church closed off the possibility of individual paths to spiritual salvation via meditation and other esoteric means which remained common in Asia and indeed in the Orthodox tradition (the Orthodox soon after refused to accept the validity of the Eighth Council). This had far-reaching consequences, one of which was to divert those spiritually seeking individuals to look for the divine outside of themselves in the world of nature and it eventually resulted in the growth of western science, which increasingly became divorced from any spirituality and fell into pure materialism. From this pernicious 'mother-soil' arose all the other 'isms' (nationalism, racism, sexism, etc), the dragon's teeth that have plagued European civilization over the last 400 years and that culminated in the madness of the two World Wars of the twentieth century.[21]

Britons are surely right to oppose the EU as a *political* project, which threatens by institutional uniformity to override the individual political and legal needs of the different European national communities, based as they are on differing paths of destiny, traditions and customs. Who have they been serving—Delors, Brittan, Andriessen and the rest? Is the new Europe to be a genuine organically functioning economic body or an economic Frankenstein, and into that body, into that vessel, what kind of spirit is seeking to incarnate?

3. Prospect for the Millennium — An Economist's View of the Disastrous Twenty-first Century*

'... those who see through these things gain a significant impression from the fact that, on the part of America, the twentieth century is introduced by the launching of certain ideas in the world via some channels of the bookselling trade serving certain movements which make use of occult means.'

Rudolf Steiner, 17 December 1916, Dornach.

At the top of the media tree

In the above quote Rudolf Steiner was clearly referring to American publications, books and magazines, which reflected the intentions and plans of the western secret brotherhoods connected to the Anglo-American establishment. Some of the most powerful men in the twentieth century have been Anglo-American media moguls, many of whom have been members of the same think tanks, such as the sister organizations the Council on Foreign Relations and the Royal Institute of Foreign Affairs, and other global special interest groups such as the Bilderberger Group and the Trilateral Commission. While they may affect rivalry from time to time, those in the British and American leading media organs operate closely in sync with each other and share similar views and values. A good example of this 'synergy' can be seen in the Rockefeller-dominated CFR journal *Foreign Affairs* and *The Economist* of London, which has been linked with Rothschild interests.

---

* Written during 1994–95.

The British print media has its own hierarchy. At the bottom are the tabloids, read by millions of voters, most of whom are little interested in abstruse questions of foreign policy about faraway countries of which they know or care little. Then come the broadsheets, for the middle class readers, both conservative and liberal, who are the conscientious letter-writing supporters of the political system. The broadsheets and the tabloids appear to entertain an unfriendly contempt for each other, but the editors of the tabloids often come from the same social background as those of the broadsheets, or else they simply filter similar messages in different formats to their differing readerships. *The Times* and *The Sun* cater for different audiences but belong to the same Rupert Murdoch stable just as 90 years ago *The Times* and *The Daily Mail* belonged to the same (Northcliffe) stable. But when push comes to shove, these seemingly very different newspapers offer value judgments which are different in form only.

At the top of the British journalism tree are the really élite news organs, the weeklies and monthlies, and the most influential of them all is the hugely respected weekly *The Economist*. This is a magazine which at first sight appears to be devoted to economic affairs, but which in fact follows an agenda that has quite other aims. Launched in 1843 to support the free market campaign of the Anti-Corn Law League, it later featured among its esteemed editors the political and constitutional expert Walter Bagehot. *The Economist* today runs a regular column titled 'Bagehot' which comments on British current affairs. Its issue of 22 October 1994 discussed Walter Bagehot's views of the monarchy. A frankly élitist anti-democrat, Bagehot believed that 'the monarchy's great role was to distract the multitude from the real business of government ...' Britain already was a 'secret' republic to men of affairs, like himself, who understood how the government actually operated. 'A republic has insinuated itself beneath the folds of monarchy,' he wrote. 'It [the monarchy] acts as a disguise. It enables our real rulers to change without heedless people knowing it. The masses of Englishmen are not fit for an elective government; if they knew how near they were to it, they would be surprised, and almost tremble.'

Bagehot's paper had traditionally supported the Whig, later the Liberal, party, the party of more or less free-thinking merchants and industrialists who resented the traditional domination of the British political system by the landed aristocracy, but too few of the Whigs and Liberals were real democrats or believed in universal suffrage. By the late nineteenth century, élite private school education and membership of Freemasonic lodges had initiated many British middle class males into the élitist values and symbolic predilections of the aristocracy. Their political sentiments thus inclined many Whigs and Liberals to oligarchy, the system of government favoured by Bagehot. In 1870 Disraeli, the Tory Prime Minister, seeking to pre-empt the dangers of socialism, extended voting rights to working class men. Six years later he made Queen Victoria Empress of India, and so began the jingoistic jamboree which intoxicated the newly-enfranchised masses with the escapist delusions of imperialism. Some 20 years on, the arrival of the popular press boosted such delusions and served to anaesthetize the newly literate working classes to social conditions at home by tales of imperial glories abroad. No matter how low down you were in the social scale, there were always millions of brown-skinned savages lower down than you desperate for the benefits of the civilization with which you were associated but all too infrequently enjoyed. In this sense the Empire was indeed a disguise, and this element of 'disguise' remains a major feature of *Economist* thinking today, both in its domestic and foreign policy agendas.

For much of the twentieth century, and especially since the establishment of the overt *Mundus*, if not *Pax*,

Americanus since 1945, *The Economist* has not only been a faithful supporter of the interests of the United States (despite occasional editorial tut-tuts at certain aspects of US policy); it has been a veritable missionary journal for what could be called 'Anglo-Saxon values', the values of those who speak the English language and whose thoughts are moulded by it, not only in economic affairs but in virtually the whole spectrum of human life, from stock market behaviour patterns and corporate ownership models to the influence of MTV and the Big Mac. From the media treetop, the views of *The Economist* filter down to lower branches of the foliage; its 'Intelligence Unit' reports, for example, are widely referred to and quoted throughout the media and publishing world. The BBC happily defers to such reports instead of garnering its own information, assuming that, like itself, reporters with *The Economist* are 'disinterested professionals' whose word can be trusted.

The emergence of a new ideology: civilizationalism

Chapter 2 discussed the map that appeared in September 1990, at the height of the Gulf Crisis, in *The Economist* (hereafter *TE*) in a special feature article entitled 'A New Flag—Defence and the Democracies'. (By 'the Democracies', 'the West' and 'the international community', *TE* always means Britain and America, the English-speaking world.) The article called for a full-blown security alliance between Western Europe (the EU) and the USA, which would also be an economic and cultural alliance. In the new world of the Lukewarm Peace, the new potential enemies were seen to be a chauvinist Russia, desperate to reassert its superpower status, a resurgent unstable Germany, and fundamentalist Islam. Nothing was said about China or Japan. Above all, the article implied in various ways that Russia and Germany must be prevented from getting too close to each other. At this time, the North Atlantic Free

Trade Area (NAFTA, organized by the Clinton Administration in 1993) was hardly even a twinkle in a Round
Tabler's eye. But those who remembered how in 1984 voices
had scoffed at the idea of a realization of Orwell's night-
marish tripolar world, saying *Nineteen Eighty-Four* was
more to do with the realities of the late 40s than the 80s,
looked at the new flag on each page of the feature article
and wondered — because it was clearly the flag of the European Union incorporated into that of the United States.
This was more than an analysis of economic trends, more
even than a programme for international economic development; this article was flying a very wide-ranging and
significant kite of global and world-historical dimensions.
What became of that kite, that journalistic UFO?

In just three years, by the summer of 1993, the UFO
reappeared, this time more formidably, in the form of
another article in another magazine of the English-speaking
élite. The magazine was *Foreign Affairs*, the most influential
foreign policy studies journal in the USA, published by the
Council on Foreign Relations (CFR), itself the most influential and prestigious pressure group in the history of US
foreign policy. This bipartisan body was established after
the First World War in tandem with the formation in Britain
of the Royal Institute of International Affairs (Chatham
House) to coordinate the foreign policies of 'the Democracies' by extraparliamentary non-democratic means (i.e.
via clubs, lobby groups and personal influence). The
Council has dominated US foreign policy-making for much
of this century and has kept the USA, post-1941, on its
imperial internationalist track. Its members were prime
architects of the institutions of the *Pax Americana* era such as
the UN, IMF, World Bank, GATT, NATO, WTO, etc.

The article in question was entitled 'The Clash of Civilizations?', and the controller on the ground of this high-
flying robot was Samuel P. Huntington, Professor of the
Science of Government, Director of the John M. Olin

Institute for Strategic Studies at Harvard University and longtime prominent academic member of the CFR.[1] Huntington posited a world all too redolent of Orwell's, a world of conflicting continents, but one in which culture and religion would take the place of ideology. 'The West', meaning the US plus Western and Central Europe, would be forced to defend its interests against its rivals: Russia, Islam, and the Confucian world of East Asia. Just as the writer of the 1990 *TE* article asserted that Russia was not part of the western community, because she had missed out on the Renaissance, the Reformation and the Enlightenment, so Huntington repeated the point and declared that, in effect, Europe would again be split east and west of a line from the Baltic to Bosnia, a line which represented the historical divide between the Protestant/Catholic world and the Orthodox/Islamic world. Huntington posits a new bipolarity to replace that of the Cold War, namely, that of 'the West versus the Rest' (not his phrase), i.e. western modern nations and cultures versus non-western modern or non-modern nations.

Huntington writes that it will be in the interest of the West 'to promote greater cooperation and unity within its own civilization, particularly between its European and North American components; to incorporate into the West societies in Eastern Europe and Latin America whose cultures are close to those of the West; to promote and maintain cooperative relations with Russia and Japan ... to limit the expansion of the military strength of Confucian and Islamic states; to moderate the reduction of western military capabilities and maintain military superiority in East and South-west Asia; to exploit differences and conflicts between Confucian and Islamic states; to support in other civilizations groups sympathetic to western values and interests; to strengthen international institutions that reflect and legitimate western interests and values and to promote the involvement of non-western states in those

Western
Christianity
circa 1500

Orthodox
Christianity
and Islam

RUSSIA

FINLAND

SWEDEN

ESTONIA

LATVIA

LITHUANIA

BELA-
RUSSIA

POLAND

CZECH
REP.

SLOVAKIA

UKRAINE

SLOVENIA
HUNG.

MOLD.

CROATIA

ROMANIA

SERBIA

BULGARIA

MONTE-
NEGRO

MACEDONIA

ALB.

Black Sea

ITALY

GREECE

N

TURKEY

0 ⊢———⊣ 200
MILES

Source: W. Wallace; THE TRANSFORMATION OF
WESTERN EUROPE. London: Pinter, 1990.
Map by Ib Ohlsson for FOREIGN AFFAIRS.

*From the article by Samuel P.
Huntington in* Foreign Affairs,
Summer edition 1993

institutions.' The West, he says, will need 'to maintain the economic and military power necessary to protect its interests in relation to these civilizations.'

Huntington is writing on behalf of those who have been striving for at least a century now — from at least the time of Cecil Rhodes, John D. Rockefeller and the founding of the American Empire in the Pacific — for world domination by the English-speaking peoples. Huntington's aims are quite clear; he wishes Anglo-American culture ('the West') to dominate the world in the twenty-first century just as it has done in the nineteenth and twentieth centuries.[2]

After NAFTA, TAFTA!

Certain sections of Huntington's article need particular attention. For example, it recommended, among others, the following aim for the West: 'to promote greater cooperation and unity within its own civilization, particularly between its European and North American components'. What he is implying here in veiled terms *TE* was calling for three years earlier in more concrete fashion. Then, in its 27 May–2 June 1995 issue, *TE* upped the ante even further by running a leading editorial article arguing the need for TAFTA, a Transatlantic Free Trade Association between the EU and NAFTA: 750 million people with a gross regional economy over $15 trillion plus. We were told that, far from this being a mere flight of fancy by some economic game theorist, it had already been suggested by 'Canada', that Newt Gingrich 'wants it pursued', that 'Germany is well-disposed', that Britain 'is developing the theme' (in a speech by Douglas Hurd the previous weekend), that the 'Clinton administration is "intrigued"', and that the European Union's trade commissioner 'favours an initiative of some kind'. Obviously, the great and the good had already got something simmering here that the rest of us had not even known was on the menu. Suddenly, something that bears an uncanny resemblance to George Orwell's Oceania (from *Nineteen Eighty-Four*) rises from the pages of that menu and appears on our mental tables to be ingested.

At first, *TE*'s leader purports to find various economic reasons why TAFTA might not be such a good thing, but then comes the sleight of hand:

> ... progress on trade would surely help to cement the North Atlantic alliance ... Economics and security should go hand in hand, and the European Union ... shows that economic cooperation can lead on to a much more elaborate and cohesive joint undertaking; the EU started out, after all, as a club for coal and steel producers ... But economics and free trade are not necessarily enough. It is idle to imagine that, in a world devoid of tariffs and trade barriers, disagreements, and indeed wars, would not arise. It is equally idle to imagine that relations between North America and Western Europe can be wholly invigorated by a round of trade talks. To believe that is certainly to do less than justice to *the full range of values and interests they have in common*. [Emphasis TMB.]

Here is the shift into Huntington territory, land that was actually marked out by *TE* in its September article of five years before. Economic issues are left far behind as the leader writer peers boldly into his brave new TAFTA world:

> These values and interests reflect what is broadly a common outlook, arising from broadly the same cultural [read 'Anglo-American' — TMB] tradition and directed at broadly the same set of aims and ideals. They have been responsible for much of the world's present shape. They are not all noble or immune to criticism. But in the second part of this century they have seen off Fascism and Communism, laid the foundations for democracy in countries that had known little but despotism, and

helped to spread prosperity on a scale unsurpassed in human history.

Clearly, the unknown writer was thinking not of 'the West', but merely of America and Britain. But there is more:

If North America [a nod to Canada?] and Europe [a nod to France?] can maintain the dynamism of this shared identity, they can continue to shape the world for the better. *To do so they need not just good commercial relations but something like a shared foreign and security policy.* At a minimum, there will be threats to their shared interests. What these threats will be no one can say [although Huntington did so two years before — TMB], but some of the candidates — resurgent Russia, intolerant Islam, nuclear-armed desperado states — are closer to Europe than to America. NATO is the organization to deal with such threats, though not, to be sure, the NATO of yesterday that was designed to fight the Russians, but rather a new NATO of tomorrow. *It is towards this, not just towards TAFTA, that the allies' eyes should be turning.* [Emphasis added.]

Here then, we see the consistent presentation by *TE* of their favoured scenario for the twenty-first century: a transatlantic federation, the eastern 'borders' of which would stop at the frontiers of Eastern Orthodox countries. It is a scenario based on 'shared values and interests' just like Huntington's. And like *TE* article of 1990 it comes with a map, this time decorating the magazine's front cover to make sure we all get the point. Despite the nods to 'North America' in the leader, it is clear from the map that it is alliance with the USA which is meant, since only the USA is shaded the same as Europe. We note that the map's eastern border of Europe cuts through Bosnia, Hungary, Slovakia and Poland. Indeed, the war in Bosnia was tolerated precisely to establish this very 'cultural' demarcation line

The Economist, *27 May 1995*

between the 'western Protestant/Catholic' part of Europe and the 'Eastern Orthodox' part. America allowed the war to go on in order to manoeuvre the participants into the position where they would accept the American terms for peace. As in 1918–19, Europe submitted to America's 'disinterested peacemakers' and the lines they drew across her body. *TE* map of 1990 showed Europe split along the same cultural 'frontier', as did a map of Eastern Europe in Huntington's article.

Redwood and Rifkind inseminate the TAFTA idea

The *Sunday Telegraph* of 17 September 1995 carried a story entitled: 'Our future is with US — Redwood'. John Redwood, the defeated candidate in the Conservative party leadership election in July 1995, travelled to the USA during the summer not long after his challenge for the premiership in which the previously not very well-known Tory politician was suddenly catapulted into the media spotlight for several weeks. In America he was treated seriously as a possible prime minister. The *Sunday Telegraph* reported that he went on a 'round of the foundations and policy institutes of Washington. Mr Redwood said that he had built links that would buttress Conservatism 2000 (the new policy study group he intended to launch on 27 September) and lend it extra campaigning muscle. A series of publications was planned, co-produced with the Heritage Foundation, the brains trust of the Reagan revolution ... The *Washington Times* devoted an editorial to Mr Redwood's visit entitled "A Second Thatcher Revolution?" praising him for trying to re-establish "the kind of political relationship and exchange of ideas that made for such fertile cross-pollination during the Reagan-Thatcher years".' What was the big idea Redwood brought back with him from the US, the idea with which he wished to 'pollinate' British (and European?) politics? The first sentence of the *Sunday Telegraph* article reads: 'John Redwood ... is taking up the cause of a trans-atlantic common market as a radical alternative to a single European currency and "ever closer union" in Europe. The project, *which is set to be a key feature of foreign policy for his new Conservatism 2000 think tank* [emphasis TMB] has emerged from the former Welsh Secretary's visit to the US last week. In a speech planned for 27 September [NB two days before Michaelmas — TMB] Mr Redwood will propose an Atlantic free trade area based on the principles of NAFTA, the North American Free Trade Agreement, which was signed by Canada, Mexico and the US in 1994 ... Mr Redwood said last week. "The NAFTA model is a much better way to go." '

John Redwood's high public profile, created by his leadership challenge to John Major earlier in the year, guaranteed considerable media attention for his proposal, and it was thereby injected into the European debate in the UK. An idea thus floated by *TE* back in May away from the full glare of publicity (*TE*, while being highly influential, exercises its influence over the rest of the media from a discreet distance) could thus be pushed right into the spotlight.

As if to underline it still further from a seemingly opposite direction, Malcolm Rifkind, the new Foreign Secretary, chose to bring up and support, if in a more veiled and devious fashion, the same idea in his first major foreign policy speech on 21 September, delivered not in Parliament (still in recess) but at the Royal Institute of International Affairs (Chatham House), the British Establishment's foreign policy ideas factory and the partner of the Council on Foreign Relations in the USA. The media chose to gloss over this particular aspect of Rifkind's speech, focusing instead on his trumpeting of the supremacy of the 'national interest' over the claims of a 'bogus [European] unity'. However, the London *Times*, now owned by Rupert Murdoch, the international media mogul, an Australian by birth but a US citizen (as well as *The Times* for the élite, he also owns the *Sunday Times* for the middle class and *The Sun* and *The News of the World* for the masses), in its report on Rifkind's speech, included the following: 'He told the RIIA that Britain intended ... to take advantage of its unique links with America to give new life to the transatlantic relationship ... he highlighted reviving and expanding the transatlantic relationship as a strong British interest. [He] called for global trade liberalization, with Europe and America leading the way. *The goal should be transatlantic free trade but the new partnership must include a much closer dialogue between Congress and the parliaments of Western Europe.*' [Emphasis TMB].

The Times editorial described Rifkind's speech as 'a masterly debut, an honest, clear and intelligent development of Palmerston's dictum that the object of foreign policy is "the furtherance of British interests".' Lord Palmerston was the British Foreign Minister and later Prime Minister who initiated the first British attacks against the eastern powers of China (Opium Wars) and Russia (Crimean War); the guiding principle of his policy was the protection and advancement of British trade, as he wrote in 1841: 'The rivalry of European manufacturers is fast excluding our production from the markets of Europe, and we must unremittingly endeavour to find in other parts of the world new vents for the produce of our industry. The world is large enough and the wants of the human race ample enough to afford a demand for all that we can manufacture; but it is the business of the government to open and to secure the roads for the merchant.'[3]

Speaking 154 years later, Britain's Foreign Secretary, quoting Palmerston with approval in his very first words, was saying exactly the same thing: 'Last year our total assets abroad exceeded £1.4 trillion. We had a net income of over £10 billion from our investment overseas. Only the US attracts more foreign investment.' 'This explained,' said *The Times* report paraphrasing Rifkind, 'why Britain had a permanent voice in the Security Council and why a strong United Nations mattered to Britain.' As Rifkind put it, 'not because we want to be a big player for its own sake, but because we must be active wherever our national interests are at stake; and they are at stake throughout the world.' Words such as these have been used to justify British interference with the affairs of countries all over the globe for at least the last 154 years. We should remember that they exactly echo the sentiments regularly expressed in *TE*, a journal which was founded in 1843, during the time of Lord Palmerston, to further the interests of British merchants.

Rifkind was also flying a kite, in fact two kites, because he was seeking both to pre-empt John Redwood's policy document due for launch six days later, and to give a signal to the EU leaders who met at Majorca on 22–23 September to discuss Europe's future prior to the EU Intergovernmental Conference of 1996. At the Majorca meeting, the British Prime Minister John Major gave an interview to BBC Radio (23 September) in which he also made a point of endorsing new transatlantic links between the US and Europe. Such British politicians like to pretend that they are improvising in a pragmatic manner, merely responding to the constantly changing turn of events, but always in the light of 'British national interests'; it is never said who defines those 'interests'.[4]

Bosnia and Northern Ireland: Primaries for TAFTA

All this was happening during the summer and early autumn of 1995 against a background of other American moves to intervene in the destiny of Europe. In Bosnia US envoy Richard Holbrooke's 'peace plan' was 'welcomed by all' and its provisions for a 51–49% division of the multi-ethnic state were exactly and conveniently underlined on the battlefield by the advances of the armies of the Bosnian-Croat alliance which Washington had created in 1994.

The peace talks were due to be held not in Europe but in New York, for Holbrooke had set himself a deadline of 25 September to bring them about; the American Government's intentions for Bosnia were thus broadly realized by Michaelmas (29 September), and by mid-October the US-brokered ceasefire was holding. The other area of US intervention was Northern Ireland, where over the summer of 1995 there was increasing talk from both the British and Irish Governments of the need for an 'international commission' to mediate, bring the parties to the peace table and oversee the handover of weapons. It soon became clear that this 'international' commission was going to be dominated by the US. By stubbornly holding to its new found principle, enunciated only in the spring of 1995, that the IRA must begin to hand over weapons before substantive talks can begin, the British Government had created a deadlock in the peace process, a vacuum, into which the US could step, posing as the peacemaking mediator. The White House duly obliged. To near-delirious crowds in Belfast during his carefully stage-managed media blitz-visit to the province, President Clinton was sufficiently barefaced to declare: 'Blessed are the peacemakers, for they shall inherit the earth.' [Emphasis TMB.]

Both in Bosnia and in Northern Ireland, many people are so desperate for peace that they will grasp at any straws to achieve it. In this way, the occult directors of Anglo-American policy work with the element of *time*. They create situations of stress, tension and violence which are then drawn out to breaking point and beyond until people can stand no more, and, begging for peace at any price, submit to Anglo-American intentions. As *TE* put it in its leader of 23 September 1995, 'It [peace settlement in Bosnia] will weaken the idea that different peoples and religions can rub along together, but at least it will be peace.' In an article later in that issue, the *TE* writer says: the 'indigestible little rump of multi-fibred Bosnian flesh' that will be left 'will

The ceasefire line in Bosnia, September 1995

The divisions of Bosnia agreed at the Dayton, Ohio peace talks, December 1995

probably be but the palest shadow of the harmonious secular Bosnia-Hercegovina that was once held up as a beacon of enlightened tolerance in a sea of Balkan bigotry. Peace, it seems, will have come only with dismemberment and the enforcement of a greater degree of ethnic homogeneity. This price now seems widely accepted.'

TE can claim that for years it had been urging the US Government to take a firmer, tougher line in Bosnia to bring peace earlier, but since *TE* is part of the very same extended policy establishment that informs that government, it knew only too well that the Americans would not move until the time was right, the Serbs exhausted, and the Croat and Bosnian armed forces rebuilt and rearmed. It is significant that the *TE* leader of 23 September 1995 compared Bosnia's fate with that of Palestine's, and saw in it the seeds of a wider clash between the West and Islam, or between the West and Russia—the Huntington scenario again. *TE*'s frequent hand-wringing over US policy during the war was merely a cover to mask its affirmation of American intentions.

It is with great cynicism, therefore, that the *TE* leader concludes by saying that: 'The survival of a truly democratic federation, generous towards the Serbs and Croats who will form part of its reduced dominion, could expiate some of the sins of the past four years. Instead of being a byword for barbarism, Bosnia might then one day become a beacon of hope in the Balkans.' And its article on Bosnia, 'Ethnic Cleansing—Blood and Earth', in which it asks 'whether multi-ethnic countries can ever be harmonious', even ends with a paean to the USA as the best example of a real multi-ethnic country because it is based on 'shared ideals' and not 'blood and earth'. This might sound like a very 'Michaelic', cosmopolitan, even 'spiritual' conclusion, until we remember that *TE* has always promoted the 'ideals' and 'values' of one particular ethnic community.

Malcolm Rifkind himself in his Chatham House speech emphasized that 'the European Union is not a conspiracy against British interests'. According to these people, there is never any conspiracy; the word is to be avoided. There are never any hidden intentions or secret agendas — only pragmatic behaviour adjusted to the needs of the moment, or else cock-ups, mere errors. It is suggested in this book, on the contrary, that the British foreign policy Establishment has ever been working, either consciously or unconsciously via manipulation, in accordance with long-held and deeply-rooted occult intentions, and that the TAFTA-NATO plan, in its latest British form stemming from *TE* as early as September 1990, actually goes back to the time of Cecil Rhodes and his plans for an Anglo-Saxon world empire dominated by the joint state of Anglo-America.[55] In an article on Bosnia on 23 September 1995, *TE* wrote: 'The United States, Britain, and France worry that, if the Bosnians win too much land, Serbia may yet intervene; or that an overconfident Sarajevo government may withdraw its support from Mr Holbrooke's sketch of a peace plan.' The article went on to describe the percentages of the plan and then followed these words: 'Coincidentally — *or possibly, by some hidden design* [emphasis TMB] — those percentages correspond, almost exactly, to the situation on the ground.' What media organ, including *TE*, has sought to find out if there has been 'a hidden design'? we may ask. And yet, there is indeed a 'hidden design'; it is an 'open secret', which *TE* has been putting before its readers for years.

The occult purposes behind the TAFTA project

Why do these people in politics and in the media, the servants of the real men of power, wish to establish their superstate of TAFTA-NATO? As is their wont, they have already supplied us with the answer. Between the *TE* kite of

September 1990 and Huntington's aerial robot of 1993, which in turn created the space for *TE* airship proposal of May 1995, a fourth, metamorphosed kite article took to the air at the turn of 1992/93. The article described the gruesome fate awaiting much of the world (especially Russia) in the twenty-first century, and the actions of the English-speaking countries in that scenario. It is this December 1992 article which provides the key to understanding what was behind *TE* articles of 1990 and 1995, and also Huntington's article in *Foreign Affairs* of Summer 1993. This earlier 1992 article will now be analysed in some detail.

One hundred years earlier, in 1893, a shadowy figure, the occultist C.G. Harrison, gave a series of lectures to the equally shadowy Berean Society in London. He was speaking as someone intimately connected with the thinking of High Church Establishment circles in England which were themselves very well acquainted with occult matters, as Harrison's lectures on theoretical occultism testify. In lecture 2 of the series, he spoke of how 'the Russian Empire must die that the Russian people may live' and that 'the [Russian] national character will enable them to carry out experiments in Socialism, political and economical, which would present innumerable difficulties in Western Europe'.[6] He also described how the Russian or Slavonic race was 'a sub-race in its infancy'.[7] Just as Rome and then the Papacy had been the 'nurse' and the 'tutor' respectively to the Germanic races of Europe, so, he implied, the Slavs and the Russians would also need their nurse and tutor. Harrison's lecture came three years after the publication of the map of Europe in the satirical magazine *Truth*, which showed Russia as a 'desert' after the coming European war that was predicted in the magazine. *TE* map of 1990 showing Russia cut off from the rest of Europe and forming the state of 'Eurasia' appeared a hundred years after that *Truth* article. All of these documents concern themselves with the future of Russia.

The twenty-first century: a view from AD 2992

TE article in question (26 December 1992–8 January 1993) appeared over the Christmas New Year period exactly 70 years after the destruction of the First Goetheanum in Dornach, Switzerland, and also at the very same time that the Single European Market 1992 project was due to begin (1 January 1993). We recall that Rudolf Steiner had said that 'all cultural evolution of the future ... is a question of this union between Central Europe and Eastern Europe'.[8] By this he meant that the Central European cultural and spiritual impulse of the fifth post-Atlantean epoch, centred on anthroposophy and the Threefold Social Order, had to be passed on to the Eastern Slavs, who were to be the standard-bearers of the sixth epoch. The ahrimanic forces of opposition, working in the fifth epoch, predominantly but not exclusively through the English-speaking peoples, are striving both to prevent this connection being made and also to direct, to 'nurse' or to 'tutor' Russia along a different path of 'education'.

The article is in the form of an extract from a history of the world written in the year 2992, and is subtitled 'A World History, Chapter 13: The disastrous twenty-first century'. It is accompanied by three illustrations, all of which are in mock medieval illuminated manuscript style. This is a semiotic reference (no doubt Umberto Eco would have been amused!) to the well-known book by the American historian, the late Barbara Tuchman, *A Distant Mirror – The Calamitous Fourteenth Century*.[9] Tuchman's book dramatically portrayed the real disasters of Europe's 'puberty crisis' in the fourteenth century, which was in many respects truly cataclysmic. *TE* article's subtitle implies that the twenty-first century will be a similar century of calamity. This recognizes an occult truth – that 21 is in the life of the individual, just as in the life of humanity as a whole, a major marker, as 14 also is. But 21 is more than that; it is in a sense *the* major marker, because it is the age at which the human individual ego and the planetary Ego, who is Christ, incarnate into the human soul and into the earth—in the case of Christ, this time into the biosphere of the whole earth rather than the physical territory of a part of it as at Palestine 2000 years ago.

The fact that *TE* declares that the century in which mankind for the first time really becomes properly 'self-conscious' will be one of disasters is also significant when we recall that in the twenty-first century the impulse of the Archangel Michael, the Regent of our epoch (1879–2233, if, following Trithemius of Sponheim, we assume an arch-angelic period to be of 354 years' duration), will increase in power *vis-à-vis* the fading strength of the receding Gabrielic impulse (1525–1879). The impulse of an archangelic Time Regent does not suddenly stop when his epoch stops; on the contrary, it is then, and for a while during the first decades of the subsequent epoch, at a culmination. Thereafter, it slowly fades out while the impulse of the following Arch-angel fades in. The twentieth century has thus witnessed an epic struggle between the mighty, but receding, Gabrielic impulses of nationalism and heredity-bound or earth-bound thinking[10] and the incipient, as yet weak, but steadily burgeoning Michaelic force of cosmopolitanism and spiritualized thinking. The rise of British culture to world dominance took place entirely within the Regency of Gabriel, the Moon Archangel. Almost simultaneously with the beginning of the Michaelic epoch in 1879, Britain's star, in the sense of worldly power, began to wane. In the 1840s, when, according to Rudolf Steiner, a tremendous spiritual battle began in the cosmic sphere between moon and earth, a battle between Michael and the hosts of Ahriman, British power, centred on the Industrial Revolution and a materi-alistic world view, was at its height. In that decade, in 1843, *TE* first appeared.

The semiotic seal of the number 23

The rubric between the subtitle and the text of *TE* article reads: '*A World History*, by Dwight Bogdanov and Vladimir Lowell (University of California in Moscow, 640 pages or 27 sight-bites, published 2992), has one of the best accounts of democracy's post-1991 failure. Here is its Chapter 13.' This then is another jokey presentation, just as with the world map article of September 1990. What does the joke imply? It implies that America and Russia will be somehow fused by 2992 through intermarriage: Dwight and Lowell are American names, and Bogdanov and Vladimir are Russian. But note that it is not the University of Moscow in California, but rather, the other way around; America has 'colonized' Russia. In saying this, are we being too serious? Seeing something that is not there? Falling for a rich semiotic joke? The rest of the article will provide the answer.

The figures '640 pages, 27 sight-bites' seem innocuous enough, but if we add them we get 667 (666 + 1), and if we multiply them we get 23.7. The number 23 or, better said, 2 + 3 will be seen to be a key not only in this article; it regularly crops up like code in all sorts of permutations (£2.3 million, 0.23, 230,000, etc) in numerous significant places in *TE* and, indeed, throughout the media. The occult aspects of this number are profound, and this is not the place to go into them.[11] The number 23 appears immediately in the text of the article, though in a veiled way, in the second sentence: 'As Chapter 12 explained, the *three-sided War of Ideas* that had occupied most of the twentieth century ended in a sweeping victory for the once apparently doomed forces of liberalism.' The reference to Chapter 12 points back to Chapter 13 in the subtitle.

The second paragraph refers to the 'universal agreement' in 1991 that there was 'no serious alternative to free-market capitalism as the way to organize economic life'. (People in the former Communist bloc were being told at that time by the media that there were no alternatives to western-style capitalism or a return to Stalinism; there was 'no third way'.) The article continues: 'It was almost as widely agreed that multi-party democracy was the best form of politics...' The free market free-trading model of capitalism and party politics in parliament—both these social forms were 'gifts' to humanity from English-speaking culture in the nineteenth century, in the age of Gabriel. In his much-hyped book *The End of History and the Last Man* (1992) Francis Fukuyama triumphantly proclaimed the victory of these *two* quintessentially Anglo-Saxon social forms. Following Marx and perversely misinterpreting Hegel, Fukuyama declared that no essential changes were now to be expected; we had reached the borders of Utopia, and only administrative tinkering was left to us. He was saying, in effect, further social development is unnecessary; it stops with the fifth post-Atlantean epoch. No more epochal changes are required. The sixth epoch, which Steiner said would be the age of Slav cultural leadership, is thus aborted, not even stillborn. Anglo-Saxon cultural domination, which Fukuyama disguises by the motto 'liberal democracy and the market economy', and all that it implies for the spread of a hyper-materialism is to continue for ever.

The uses and misuses of history

Returning to *TE* article, the only challengers to the New Order were 'a handful of authoritarians... most of them in Muslim South-west Asia—and the old men still running China openly stood aside from *the new orthodoxy*' [emphasis TMB]. In other words, to use the language of the 1990 *TE* article, Islamistan and Confuciania. The enemy are now seen in religious terms, as Huntington saw them. 'To this ideological triumph was added... a technological advantage in the weapons of war...' Free markets, party politics

and military security — this is the triad in the world of the
Anglo-Saxon Establishment. There is no mention of cultural
or spiritual values; intelligence is dedicated not to them but
to the service of war. The writer himself delineates only two
factors: ideology (markets + parties), and military power.

TE's usual acute grasp of historical events and processes
is shown in the third and fourth paragraphs, which are
worth quoting in their entirety:

> All this was potentially a greater change in the course
> of history than Britain's defeat of Napoleonic France in
> 1815. That decided who was to be militarily dominant in
> the nineteenth century, but it did not put an end to the
> ideological fallacy that had begun in France in 1789 and
> reappeared in new shape in Russia in 1917. The events of
> 1989-91 could also have proved more decisive than the
> victory of the Reformation in the seventeenth century.
> That changed the ideological scene, but it did nothing to
> decide the military and political balance of power in
> Europe.
>
> Perhaps not since the battle of Actium in 31 BC, which
> made possible the *Pax Romana* of the next two centuries,
> had there been such a chance to remake the world; and in
> AD 1991, unlike 31 BC, the central idea on which the
> remaking would have been based was the victors' belief
> in every man's right to political and economic freedom.

Here it is implied that the 'ideological fallacy' of the French
Revolution was Socialism, and, in a sense, it was in that the
upper classes suffered the wrath of the lower classes as they
did after 1917 in Russia. But the French Revolution was
primarily a bourgeois revolution, and despite the sans-
culottes, it remained bourgeois; Robespierre's attempt to
enthrone his exotic Masonic Supreme Being of Reason — a
concept far removed from the concerns of the sans-
culottes — testified to that. The real ideological fallacy of the
Revolution was not socialism, which was forged not in

France but in the heat of the Industrial Revolution in England. It was nationalism; this was the germ spread by the French Revolution throughout Europe. But until Stalin's attempt to forge socialism in one country, nationalism was not the mainspring of events in Russia post-1917.

Then comes the truly insightful fourth paragraph. A direct link is suggested between *Pax Americana* and *Pax Romana*: the two world empires of their time, the two world empires at the time of the First and the Second Coming of Christ. Here is a direct link to the statements of the English occultist Harrison in 1893 about the nursing role of the Roman Empire. And not only that, for the date and the event referred to by *TE* — the Battle of Actium, where Octavian defeated Cleopatra and Mark Antony — is deeply significant in that it marked the end of the Roman Republic and the beginning of Rome's assumption of world *imperium*. The period just before and around the time of Christ thus marked Rome's failure to uphold its cultural-historical mission in the fourth post-Atlantean epoch (the development of law, politics, individual citizenship) and the beginning of its long slide backwards into the imperial, Asiatic and theocratic habits of the third epoch. In terms of power, Rome carried all before it for a time after Actium; in terms of culture and spirit, it was to sink into an abyss of decadence. At the end of *TE* sentence quoted above we see again the twofold principle: 'every man's right to political and economic freedom'. Just as under the Roman Empire, there is to be no *spiritual freedom* in the age of the *Pax Americana*. If one did not recognize the Emperor as God, the consequences were dire. What will the consequences be if one fails to acknowledge the fiats and pronouncements issued from Capitol Hill and the White House, from Wall Street, the Federal Reserve, from Hollywood and CNN?

TV news pictures of the White House often show the Egyptian obelisk standing behind it. This is powerful subliminal symbology being conveyed to the watching masses.

It says: '*We* are the inheritors of the third epoch (obelisk) and the fourth epoch (classical facade of the White House).' America's own symbolic power architecture — its contribution to the architecture of the fifth epoch — is, of course, the skyscrapers of the Manhattan skyline, which are themselves a brutal metamorphosis of the overpowering massiveness of Egyptian architecture and the static and repetitive symmetries of the Greek. In May 1942, Norman Davis, then secretary of the State Department's security subcommittee of the Advisory Committee on Post-war Foreign Policy, said that 'the British Empire as it existed in the past will never reappear and that the United States will have to take its place'. General George V. Strong, who sat on the same committee, stated that the United States 'must cultivate a mental view toward world settlement after this war which will enable us to impose our own terms, amounting perhaps to a *Pax Americana*.'[12] Both men were CFR members; Davis was CFR President at the time.

The inversion of threefolding

The historical parallels of the fourth paragraph in *TE* article are followed by a shocking reversion to the present in the three sentences of the fifth: the glowing post-1991 prospect of *Pax Americana* is stated to have rapidly faded. 'The twenty-first century became the "century of disasters", and it was not until the 2300s that it began to be possible to reassemble the beginnings of today's General Confederation of Democracies.' The twenty-first century is to be even more calamitous than the twentieth! The reference to the 2300s is noteworthy, not only because here is the number 23 again, but because the Age of Michael proper will end in approximately 2233 (1879 + 354). The entire Age of Michael is thus said to be an age of calamity. Then comes the 'General Confederation of Democracies' — a cover phrase for 'world government'. This 'began' to emerge in the 2300s and was, we presume, fully operative in the 2900s. It thus took some 600 years to come about—hardly likely given the probable pace of technological change, etc. No, the writer here wanted to focus on the 2300s for his own reasons, which, we have suggested, were those mentioned above. The final sentence presents a threefold inversion of spiritual knowledge: 'The post-1991 failure happened because of a failure of clear thinking, a failure of imagination and a failure of will.'

In what sense was this an inversion of spiritual knowledge? Before investigating this, we should note that the argument used by *TE* writer is typical of Anglo-Saxon thinking. Instead of saying, 'Don't do A, B is a better and more creative solution to the problem,' what is said is, 'If you do A, the following horrendous scenario will result.' 'Don't do A,' is not said, and neither is any creative thinking put forward as an alternative to A. One sees this approach daily in English-speaking countries—in advertisements, in TV dramas, films and documentaries. The implied message is: 'If you do this, that will happen to you.' The result is that only destructive images tend to be put before people—images of pain, breakdown, dissension—and no constructive way forward is shown. In Christian terms, it is the Crucifixion without the Resurrection; in Shakespearean terms, it is *Hamlet* without *The Tempest*. Although the article therefore purports to chronicle the collapse of the New World Order, it is the maintenance of the New World Order with which it is actually concerned, and we shall see that, in fact, the New World Order is intended to be a World Disorder, manipulated by the occult forces of the English-speaking countries for their own purposes.

The sixth paragraph, describing the collapse of the New Order, is headed 'Pillar by pillar it fell'. It suggests that the victorious New World Order forces of 1991 were three: the US, the EC and Japan. Actually, of course, Japan was anything but an equal partner. It has since the Second World

War been effectively a colony, which America, or rather, the élite forces controlling America have used to their own advantage. In 1990–91, for example, they used it to pay much of the cost of the preparations for the Gulf War. They have also used it these last 30 years to seed the materialism of industrial culture throughout East Asia, and particularly in China. South Korea, Taiwan and Hong Kong were all to a large extent enabled to get on their industrial feet by Japanese finance, know-how and example. They in turn, as well as Japan herself, have provided much of the same for mainland China's spectacular economic growth since the late 80s.[13]

The inclusion of Japan in 'the victorious coalition' points rather to the influence of the Trilateral Commission (TC), which, as a US-inspired body, the brainchild of David Rockefeller in the early 70s, has sought to manipulate world affairs by a series of regular clandestine meetings between leading politicians, businessmen, academics and others, the details of which are never reported by the world's media. Just as a similar organization, the Bilderberger Group, was established in 1954 to tie Europe to the USA, so in the early 70s, with the rise of Japan's burgeoning economy, it was felt that Japan needed binding in the same way. The Trilateral Commission is a perversion of global threefoldness, because it seeks to maintain control of global affairs by a council representing élite groups from the USA, Western Europe and Japan. Zbigniew Brzezinski, of Polish extraction and a Rockefeller protégé and National Security adviser in the TC-dominated administration of President Jimmy Carter (1976–80), was closely involved with Rockefeller in setting it up and he has been consistently working for its aims ever since.

The Japanese are seen in fact by the Anglo-American Establishment only as 'honorary whites', just as they were seen in South Africa during the apartheid regime. So to imply that there are three pillars is misleading; in fact, there are only two: the USA and Britain (plus its white Commonwealth partners), the English-speaking powers. The occult link between them has traditionally been Freemasonry, that quintessentially British creation.[14] Freemasonry was the original Internet, the original Super-highway to élite power and influence in the Anglo-American world. It may well be asked whether the 'pillars' mentioned are actually an oblique reference to Jachin and Boaz, the twin pillars of the Temple of Solomon and of every Freemasonic lodge.

The sixth and seventh paragraphs detail the collapse of the triumvirate of the USA, EC and Japan owing to economic rivalries: 'By 2006, the year of the last American military withdrawal from Europe and Asia, the coalition had collapsed.' In trade, 'by the end of the (twentieth) century there was virtually no rule book at all. The

David Rockefeller, CFR chairman and former President, Chase Manhattan Bank

Freemasons' Hall, London, built 1927–33

disruption of trade hurt the rich of the world; but it hurt the poor even more, because in the trade war that followed they were defenceless.' In 1992 — 93 the media were wondering whether the GATT system would survive, but thanks largely to the efforts of the strategically placed EU Commissioner Leon Brittan, and of another English-speaker, GATT chairman Graham Sutherland, GATT survived and metamorphosed into the World Trade Organization (WTO). In a real threefold world, this could actually become a genuine global economic forum, but like GATT, the IMF and the UN, it looks more like being a tool in the hands of the Trilateral Commission and other such Anglo-American controlled groups with hidden agendas.

The eighth paragraph brings us to a certain octave, because here emerges the global inversion of a threefold world, namely, a threefold world at war with itself. A deeper problem than economic rivalry, nationalism, is said to have led to continentalism, or hyper-nationalism. 'The hoped-for new world order [hoped for by whom, we may ask] broke up into the European Restoration, the China-Japan Co-operation Sphere, and the New Americanism.' We are at the halfway house between *TE* article of September 1990 and Huntington's article of summer 1993. This is the world of Orwell's *Nineteen Eighty-Four* with its three global superpowers of Oceania, Eurasia and Eastasia. The names in *TE* article have been carefully chosen for their subliminal nuances. 'Restoration' recalls the Restoration of Charles II after the experiment of the Commonwealth in seventeenth-century England, or the 'Restoration' of the Bourbons in France after Napoleon, in other words, something reactionary, conservative, backward-looking and timid. 'Cooperation Sphere' obviously recalls the Japanese-dominated Co-Prosperity Sphere of the Second World War, only this time the Chinese will be on top. Despite Japan's purported role in the 'victorious coalition', we notice that it is the China-Japan Co-operation Sphere and not the other way around.

Only America is given the name 'New', which implies 'forward-looking', although we shall see that that is not what is meant. So here again is another kind of threefoldness: backward-looking, looking in at each other, and forward-looking. This threefold continentalism is actually an extension of the force of nationalism from the Age of Gabriel onto the world stage in the Age of Michael. It is a perversion of the cosmopolitan Michaelic impulse: '... the force that had given birth to nationalism in the eighteenth and nineteenth centuries had now moved on to a larger stage.'

This failure to deal with economic rivalries or with nationalism is described as 'a failure of thinking', but it is not made clear why it should be so described, or how the failure of thinking differs from the failure of imagination with which the next paragraph deals. Secondly, the failure of imagination is ascribed to Europe, and the failure of will to America. Here, too, we see occult knowledge, because the American continent is the world's will, as Asia is the world's thinking (as the traditional saying *ex oriente lux* has it, wisdom, like the sun, comes from the East), and Europe-Africa the world's heart-imagination.[15] We note that the failure of thinking is not ascribed to Japan, but to all three members of the coalition. This is surely because it is not wished to suggest that Japan was doing the thinking for the coalition (it was, of course, being done in the West, but was of metabolic nature).[16]

We have come to the end of the first page of the three page article. Its last paragraph begins to discuss Europe's failure of imagination'. But on this first page, there is also the first, and the largest, of the article's three illustrations. In mock mediaeval style it shows a map of Europe with its eastern half in flames, and with a snaking vine proceeding from Germany up over the ocean to the USA along which Uncle Sam is retreating with his military hardware back to his homeland. The subliminal message is: 'When Uncle Sam leaves Europe/Germany, Eastern Europe will go up in flames.' How is this elaborated in the text?

It is said that the West Europeans concentrated on deepening, not extending the European Union. They thus excluded Eastern Europe and condemned 'Poland, Hungary and Bohemia — which with help might have managed the leap to democratic capitalism — to a long period of economic and political disorder.' It is always these three predominantly Catholic countries which the Anglo-Americans (Thatcher, Kissinger, Brzezinski, *et al.*) are concerned about. And why? Because the West Slavs and the Magyars of Central Europe are those who mediate between Western Europe and the Orthodox world of the East Slavs. It is desired by the Anglo-American West and their allies in France and the Vatican to exclude the Orthodox world from Europe and

prevent any healthy spiritual-cultural connection being made between Russia and Germany; they thus harp on about the need for Poland, Hungary and the Czech Republic to join NATO and the EU as soon as possible. Bulgaria, Romania, Serbia, Albania: these can go to the wall.[17]

Then it is said that 'the subsequent horrors in the ex-Soviet Union were perhaps too huge for anyone to halt; but Western Europe could at least have built a barrier, from the Baltic to the Black Sea, between itself and the chaos in Russia.' In the *Truth* map of 1890, Russia was to become a 'desert', in 1993, 'horrors and chaos' — this is what awaits Russia according to *TE*. Here all too clearly there is the suggestion of another wall of containment around Russia. No matter that since 1989, and in the current debate about the extension of NATO to the east, western politicians have been constantly saying, as Malcolm Rifkind said again on 21 September 1995, that Russia must not be made to feel excluded; a kind of exclusion is precisely what is being planned for her, and the true intentions of the western élites are allowed to slip out in bizarre forms, such as this backwards-looking history of the twenty-first century written in 2992.[18] Indeed, the barrier has already been built in the form of the bogus states of Belarus, Ukraine and Moldova, the sovereignty and independence of which, western spokesmen are constantly reiterating, must be defended, by NATO if necessary, against any Russian imperial revanchism.

'...the anarchy in the East spread to the borders of Germany; and by 2008 free Europe was a barely bigger place than it had been in 1988.' At the time the article was written in 1992 plans for the incorporation of the three largely Catholic states of Poland, Hungary and Bohemia into the EU and NATO were already underway, so 'the anarchy in the east' will not include Poland. Poland is too important to both the Vatican and Washington for that to be allowed.[19] Yugoslavia and Russia are a different matter. We have already seen how America's carefully laid plans for

Bosnia are working out to conform with the *TE*-Huntington design for a divided Europe. It is not clear from the text whether Eastern Europe in 2008 will be unfree because of a reassertion of Russian control or because of native authoritarian governments, but it is said plainly that by 2008 the peoples of Eastern Europe will again be spiritually and culturally oppressed, just as they were during the Cold War. The responsibility for all this, it is said, lies with Western Europe and its 'failure of imagination'. Again, this is to assume that Europe, like Japan, is independent of the US, a free agent, but since 1945, *when it comes to key areas of policy*, this has never been so. If the Western Europeans exclude the Eastern Slavs, it will be because the Anglo-American élite and their occult masters, as well as their rivals and sometime allies in the Vatican, wish them to do so.

After the three paragraphs dealing with 'the failure of thinking', and the three dealing with 'the failure of imagination', the text moves in the twelfth, thirteenth, and fourteenth paragraphs to discuss America's 'failure of will'. The US is described as having, among other things, 'an ability to see the world as a whole'. This refers, of course, only to the élite of the political Establishment, since, in many respects, the USA is like a huge island, and many ordinary Americans are, despite their TV-saturated information culture, no more knowledgeable of the rest of the world than people in any other country. 'The optimists believed that the exhilaration of the twentieth century, when the United States had twice saved the world for democracy, would rescue Americans from a return to the isolationism they had chosen for themselves in the nineteenth century and that America would once again be their saviour.' Who are these 'optimists'? None other than *TE*, of course, and their political allies in the UK. Ever since the days when Rudyard Kipling sent his 'White Man's Burden' poem to Theodore Roosevelt, a prominent section of the British Establishment have been massaging the ego of America, willing to play the part of Greek helots to America's Rome.[20]

The thirteenth paragraph declares that 'the optimists were wrong', because the USA did in fact withdraw into isolationism in the 21st century, beset by 'economic and racial troubles ... by the end of the [twentieth] century, introversion had won. The Buchanan Doctrine of 2003 — enunciated to Congress 180 years to the day after President Monroe's earlier declaration of the self-sufficiency of the Americas — made America's twenty-first century a new version of its nineteenth century. The twentieth had been only a marvellous aberration.'(!)

Here again we have the number 23: 2003. The Monroe Doctrine was announced in 1823.[21] 'The Buchanan Doctrine' doubtless points to Pat Buchanan, the right-wing, America First, fiercely Catholic politician. At the time of writing, an increasing number of commentators in the US and the UK are beginning to see him as a serious candidate for President or President-in-waiting of the United States. *TE*, of course, officially opposes him and implies it would prefer the moderate Republican candidacy of General Colin Powell, 'hero' of the Gulf War. But since the scenario sketched in the article in question is in fact one that *TE* would not at all mind seeing come about, Buchanan would be just the man to make it happen. His staunchly conservative Catholic connections and credentials would, furthermore, create a stronger bond between the Vatican and the White House, between the old Papacy of the fourth post-Atlantean epoch and the new Papacy of the fifth epoch.

After its reacceptance by the Papacy shortly before 1823,[22] the Jesuit Order immediately set about establishing itself in the USA where it now has a considerable presence, including, of course, the diplomats' university of Georgetown, where William J. Clinton was educated by Jesuits before being sent as a Rhodes Scholar to Oxford. The

Reagan-John Paul II covert campaign of collaboration (as 'revealed' graphically by *Time* magazine ten years later, 24 February 1992) to support Solidarnosc and destabilize the Polish Communist regime in the 80s could well be taken as recent proof of Steiner's indications, as could the Vatican and White House manoeuvrings with regard to Bosnia and Croatia.

The fourteenth paragraph describes how isolationist America 'took a few decades to ... sort out its internal problems. But by the mid-2000s the western hemisphere as a whole was tranquil, fairly prosperous and almost wholly democratic—an undogmatic association of free-trading nations protected by its encircling oceans (and the nuclear armoury of the United States) *from the turmoil elsewhere.*' [Emphasis TMB.] In other words, the western hemisphere became NAFTA, which was to be the great political hot potato of 1993 in the US, and for the establishment of which the energy and talents of 'youngsters' Bill Clinton and Vice-President Al Gore were exercised to the full. Indeed, historians may well come to see NAFTA as *the* achievement of the first Clinton presidential term, even its *raison d'être*. NAFTA is even referred to in the fourteenth paragraph as 'Pan-American Free Trade Area'. In the fourteenth paragraph, this contented NAFTA then turns into a larger version of nineteenth-century liberal free-trading England, protected by its own Channel and its own world-spanning Royal Navy battle fleets. Its 'encircling oceans' turn it, in fact, into Orwell's 'Oceania' of *Nineteen Eighty-four*. America being, as far as *TE* is concerned, the near-perfect model for the world, the model which, despite a few warts, is basically sound, the US-dominated American hemisphere's destiny in the twenty-first century is seen as being 'tranquil ... prosperous ... democratic ... undogmatic'—the kind of prospect held out for humanity in Francis Fukuyama's infamous tome of 1992, *The End of History and the Last Man*.[23]

So, peace and prosperity in the Americas, but turmoil

The Old Roman Empire aids the New – Reagan and Pope John Paul II in 1982

Cover of Time *magazine, 24 February 1992*

everywhere else. The subliminal message is 'Follow the American Way'. The next section of the text goes on to chronicle the disasters that befell those regions which chose not to ride the American Superhighway. UN action in Somalia in the 1990s, it is said, was successful, but the last action of its kind. In January 1993, the Americans had only just gone into Somalia, and so *TE*, true to form, is here predicting a triumphant outcome for its heroes. The Somalians, however, had other ideas, as we now know, and America was forced to beat a retreat with egg on its face. It is noteworthy that the text says that the UN (i.e. US-led forces) 'administered the place until the election of the governments for the two countries into which the Somalians decided to divide themselves'. This has normally been the case wherever the US has established its *Pax Americana*. Lines are drawn and, once multi-ethnic communities are separated into more rigid ethnic units, there is division of one into two or reduction of three into two.

Another such division comes in the next paragraph: 'After the failure in Yugoslavia, Western Europe began to lower a mental curtain between itself and events east of Vienna.' We have seen that in September 1990 *TE*, and later in 1993 Huntington, were actually advocating just such a lowering of 'mental curtains' in the name of 'culture and religion'. The implication is clear: Europe is to be divided in two again! To reinforce the notion, the unknown writer concludes the paragraph by saying: '...the doctrine that sovereignty permitted any abuse of human rights—*cuius regio, eius potestas*—took new root.' This refers back semiotically to the Peace of Westphalia in 1648 which sealed the Thirty Years' War and the religious division of Europe with the formula of *cuius regio, eius religio*. (lit. 'whose rule, his religion'; i.e. the prince shall decide the religion). We recall that Huntington later argued that the world would now divide especially on religious lines. *TE* writer's statement is also cynical in the extreme, because *TE* has frequently played down demands that countries like, say, China, do more on human rights, arguing that greater economic growth will do more to further such rights. For the non-Christian *TE*, of course, *potestas* (power) has replaced *religio*. The forces behind *TE* are actually striving for world government via the UN, so for them it is vital to establish the UN's right to interfere in the affairs of sovereign states. This might seem to contradict what was said above about human rights, but it does not. *TE* and its allies oppose 'internationalist' meddling concern about human rights when it suits them, i.e. in countries where major capitalist investment is being made, but support internationalist interventions in other countries, such as Iraq, when different Anglo-American interests are at stake.

Conventional news media in the West have already done a good job in spreading the idea that anyone who speaks of the danger of 'one world government via the UN' is either a semi-crazed gun-toting member of crypto-Fascist American militias or else is sympathetic towards them. This is because so little is revealed by western media about the men, the ideas and the process behind the formation of the UN. If one takes the trouble to probe a little deeper into these, it soon becomes clear what the aims of those men were. Those who conceived of the UN, and of the League of Nations before it, were the same men who either belonged to or stood close to the Council on Foreign Affairs in America and its sister organization, the Royal Institute of International Affairs (Chatham House) in Britain. Before these two organizations were formally founded after the First World War, those men shared the world view of the Round Table organization founded by Cecil Rhodes, first as a secret and then as a semi-secret society dedicated to establishing a world system under Anglo-American control. They believed that the English-speaking peoples were 'the finest race in the world, and that the more of the world [they] inhabit, the better it is for the human race'. The British members of the Round

Table, acting out of a lofty and idealistic Victorian imperialistic spirit which was thoroughly permeated by the tenets of Social Darwinism had as their one aim and object

> ... the extension of British rule throughout the world, the perfecting of a system of emigration from the United Kingdom and colonization of all lands wherein the means of livelihood are attainable by energy, labour and enterprise, and especially the occupation by British settlers of the entire continent of Africa, *the Holy Land* [emphasis TMB], the valley of the Euphrates, the islands of Cyprus and Candia, the whole of South America, the islands of the Pacific not hitherto possessed by Great Britain, the whole of the Malay Archipelago, the seaboard of China and Japan, the ultimate recovery of the United States of America as an integral part of the British Empire, the inauguration of a system of Colonial Representation in the Imperial Parliament, which may tend to weld together the disjointed members of the Empire [herein lay the seeds of the League and the UN — TMB], and finally the foundation of so great a power as to hereafter render wars impossible and promote the best interest of humanity.[24]

There have of course been many genuine idealists and pacifists who have responded positively to the idea of a League of Nations and of the United Nations but who were loath to any notions of imperial or nationalist domination by the English-speaking peoples. Such well-meaning people were used by the Rhodes group as a cover to further their aims. Those people were responding to the subconscious promptings of the new cosmopolitan impulse of the Archangel Michael which had been making its way into the stream of history since 1879. The forces of opposition recognize the inevitability of this impulse and work with it to bend it to their own purposes, hence all the noble idealistic words spoken in connection with the UN, which far from being a genuine assembly of the nations of the world agreeing together is an assembly dominated by an oligarchy of the five permanent members. In three of these, the USA, Britain and France, Freemasonry has been influential in élite circles for over 200 years. The very land for the UN was donated by John D. Rockefeller II, after Nelson Rockefeller had originally suggested the UN should be sited in the Rockefeller Center, and the monolithic UN building was designed by a Rockefeller architect, Wally Harrison, a man in Nelson Rockefeller's inner circle. The Rockefellers have been closely associated with the CFR since its founding in 1921; one of the key figures in its establishment was the Morgan finance house lawyer and Rockefeller trustee J.W. Davis. The original headquarters of the CFR, Pratt Mansion, was bought for the CFR by John D. Rockefeller II. Throughout the 1950s and 60s David Rockefeller was Vice-President of the CFR: 'He was a guardian of the establishment center, a fixed point of its moral order, not so much an architect or executor as a trustee of its informed and concentrated will.'[25]

While some members of the British élite were adamant that Britain should not be supplanted by the USA, the more realistic members understood that Britain's power base was too fragile and that the worldwide British Empire, founded on overt military power, was destined to give way to the more economically based American world empire. Such liberal imperialists therefore cooperated in this transfer of power, seeking to play Greece to America's Rome and thus continue to exert an influence over US policies, while the more unregenerate right wing conservative members of the British élite were bitterly anti-American and resented the American take-over in all its manifestations, cultural as well as military and economic. Thus the conservative thinker Roger Scruton has claimed that 'the British Empire lives on in America, just as the Roman Empire lived on in Byzantium, although in a form more vital, more industrious and more generous'. During World War II, Harold Macmillan, later Conservative Prime Minster (1956–63), said to Richard Crossman, later a member of the Labour Cabinet (1966–70): 'We, my dear Crossman, are Greeks in this American Empire. You will find the Americans much as the Greeks found the Romans—great big, vulgar, bustling people, more vigorous than we are and also more idle, with more unspoiled virtues but also more corrupt. We must run Allied Forces Headquarters as the Greek slaves ran the operations of the Emperor Claudius.' (Quoted in Hitchens, op. cit., p. 23.) The irony here—perhaps intended—is that it was under the Emperor Claudius that Rome conquered Britain. Winston Churchill at first resisted Britain's going into 'imperial receivership' at America's hands; he finally bowed to the inevitable. In conversation with Clark Clifford on the way to make his famous Iron Curtain speech at Fulton, Missouri, a world-weary Churchill confessed that 'America has now become the hope of the world. Britain has had its day. At one time we had dominions all over the world ... But England is gradually drying up. The leadership must be taken over by the United States. You have the country, the people; you have the democratic spirit, the natural resources which England has not ... If I were to be born again, I'd want to be born an American.'[26]

The important point to bear in mind here is that Ahriman, who works through the western occult brotherhoods whose tools organizations such as the CFR, the RIIA, the UN, are, is not at all interested in Britain and the USA *per se*. He is no nationalist or patriot. He is interested in global power, turning the world into a global slave state in which humanity will forget all about any spiritual world or spiritual concepts. Ahriman desires to work primarily through the English-speaking peoples in this fifth post-Atlantean epoch because he knows that they bear a particular affinity to that part of the human entelechy which has to be developed in this epoch, namely, the Consciousness Soul, the will to the good. About this, Rudolf Steiner said that the secret western brotherhoods

> do not work out of any particular British patriotism, but out of the desire to bring the whole world under the yoke of pure materialism ... Those who know what impulses are at work in world events can also steer them. No other national element, no other people, has ever before been so usable as material for transforming the whole world into a materialistic realm. Therefore, those who know want to set their foot on the neck of this national element and strip it of all spiritual endeavour — which, of course, lives equally in all human beings. Just because karma has ordained that the Consciousness Soul should work here particularly strongly, the secret brotherhoods have sought out elements in the British national character. Their aim is to send a wave of materialism over the earth and make the physical plane the only valid one. A spiritual world is only to be recognized in terms of what the physical plane has to offer. This must be opposed by the endeavours of those who understand the necessity of a spiritual life on earth.[27]

In 1993, trading blocs were much in the news: the EU, NAFTA, and the possible collapse of the American-inspired GATT. It did not collapse then, of course; by April 1994 it was re-cobbled together and later recast as the World Trade Organization. But the article implies that its days were numbered and that the consequence was greater world poverty and the spread of dictatorship. The fact that since 1945 successive US governments have supported a whole bevy of execrable regimes around the world is ignored. 'By 2030 a larger proportion of the world's population was living under authoritarian rule than half a century earlier.' Such is the grim prospect held out before us.

A new giant of the twenty-first century: China

The reference to 23 is immediately followed by another in the succeeding paragraph, the 20th, which introduces the two giants of the next three centuries: 'Out of this confusion arose two new great powers, which between them came to dominate the twenty-second and twenty-third centuries.' Here is a double reference; not only is 23 mentioned by itself, but 23 is implicit in 22–23. We recall that the Michael Age will come to an end in about 2233 (354 years on from 1879), so the period of dominance by the 'two new great powers' will span the rest of the Michael Age. It is significant that, while the article is said to be written from the vantage point of the thirtieth century, the action described in it here goes no further than the twenty-third century, and in fact most of the dated action takes place before the 2030s, i.e. very close to today. The fifth paragraph had stated that 'today's [i.e. thirtieth century's] General Confederation of Democracies' began in the 2300s. From then until the thirtieth century apparently nothing of interest happened. The point here is that the writer surely wished to focus on the number 23.

The two new giants turn out to be the two powers which *TE* in September 1990 and Samuel P. Huntington later in 1993 were presenting as leading potential threats to the hegemony of the 'West', namely, China and an Islamic superstate or Confederation.[28] China, it says, 'continued to *grow faster than any other big country*, sometimes by a margin of *two* or *three* percentage points a year [emphasis TMB]. Since it had over a billion people, that made it a great economic power by the 2020s . . .' Interestingly enough, nothing is said about China's take-over of Hong Kong in 1997 – a major potential trouble spot for the British Establishment. But Taiwan is said to be reabsorbed after 'a deal' in 2007 and China 'settled down to be a market economy under an authoritarian political leadership'. The choice of the words 'settled down' perhaps indicates that this is precisely what has been desired for China by the Anglo-American élites who have played, through investments made by their Asian surrogates in Hong Kong, Singapore, Taiwan and Tokyo, as well as directly by their own not inconsiderable investments, a major role in 'wet-nursing' China's transition from Communism to capitalism.

China, it is said, will bully Japan, by detonating a nuclear warhead over the sea off Yokohama, into becoming China's Switzerland, 'a rich, efficient provider of specialized financial and business products.' Here we have an example of the grossest kind of cynicism—firstly, because there are said to have been 'no casualties, except for the *unlucky* [emphasis TMB] crew of a tanker that had ignored the warnings'. This recalls the Japanese fishing boat *Lucky Dragon No. 5* that suffered the same fate during the detonation of an American H-Bomb off Bikini atoll on 1 March 1954; 23 members of the crew died from the radioactive fallout. Once again, innocent Japanese seamen die as a result of Big Power machinations. The rulers of the English-speaking world have wanted to gain control over China since at least the end of the nineteenth century when America began to see its 'manifest destiny' in domination of the Pacific. America's attempts to dominate the Asia-Pacific Economic Community (APEC) are but the continuation of this drive, to which the TAFTA project has now been added in order to cement American control over the world's three leading economic regions.

The second reason why the statement about Japan's approaching fate as economic concubine of China is so cynical is that the Rulers of the West would appear to have decided that Japan has outlived its usefulness; it is China and its colossal population that they have always had their sights on. Japan, since the American Commodore Perry forced it to open at gunpoint in 1853–54 and Britain entered into alliance with it in 1902–22, has merely been used as a means to an end. The Rulers of the West saw that the energies of the people of Japan, severely disciplined and inured to hardship and submission by the centuries-long rule of the *samurai* military class, would be the most suitable instrument for initiating the process of materialistic modernization in East Asia, and through their 'tutelage' of Japan, first by America, then by Britain, and then by America again, they have achieved their aim admirably. Japan was the model which all the rising economies of East Asia have sought to emulate. Singapore is now held up as an example of an efficient, dynamic, super-modern state from which we can all learn. Japan, its role effectively played out, is cursorily assigned to the status of administrative mandarin in the new Chinese Empire.

However, *TE* may be up to another game here. In describing this scenario, which amounts to a huge and humiliating loss of face for the Japanese *vis-à-vis* their Chinese rivals for power in Asia,[29] *TE* may be calculating that its Japanese readers, of whom there are many in the business world, will draw the opposite conclusion and press for rapid progress in Japan's nuclear war fighting capacity to prevent any such Chinese nuclear blackmail. Indeed, the prospect of Japan nuclear-armed, but, like Britain, still under America's thumb, as the leader of an Asian bloc wary of, if not hostile to, a resurgent China is the kind of fear and anxiety-ridden scenario in which ahrimanic forces function best. Peoples can then be played off against one another. The situation in East Asia will then resemble that intended for Europe: two massive and threatening imperial states, Russia and China, will be opposed by a US-dominated alliance of other states in their regions led by the nuclear-armed US puppet states, Britain and Japan.

This is not necessarily to contradict what was said earlier about the ultimate intentions of Anglo-American ruling groups with regard to China. With a quarter of the world's

From The Economist, *December 1992*

population, that country will inevitably determine the course of events in the next century, for continuing modernization there on a massive scale would inexorably lead to the destabilization and depletion of the world's resources and consequent catastrophic global crisis. Such a global crisis happened before, 700 years ago, with another eruption of Mars forces in the shape of the Mongol invasions.[30] That 700-year rhythm recurs, its cyclicity is doubtless known to the Rulers of the West and they make their plans accordingly. Rudolf Steiner indicated that the hidden effect of the Mongol invasions was to force the Europeans to discover America as a psychological (ahrimanizing) balance to the atavistic, earth-denying (luciferic) influences of the Mongols.[31] Are we now in for a reversal of this process? Since the 1840s, Britain and America have been forcing the Mars people, the Mongoloid race, violently into the stream of world development in the fifth epoch. The effect of the ahrimanization of Mongoloid culture and society may well be to destabilize life on earth to such a point that a solution will be sought in escape from the planet via the space travel that has been developed predominantly in the New World. A new Age of Discovery will be hailed as the panacea for earth's problems. Already, Americans are talking about 'seeding' Mars and making it fit for human habitation. Japanese finance is being sought for NASA's Mars projects, since the Americans are no longer wealthy enough to pay for them alone. The earth's unique position in the cosmos as the Body of Christ will be ignored and denied if such ideas and projects gain ground.

A new giant of the twenty-first century: 'Islamistan'

Returning to *TE* article, 'the other new great power of the twenty-first century' is presented as having first emerged 1400 years ago. We thus have the re-emergence of a Mongoloid-induced global crisis after 700 years, the re-emergence of Islamic world power after 1400 years, both in the twenty-first century: 7–14–21, all in the same para-graph. Here again is reference to an occult principle that works in biography, in fact in all time processes — the law of seven. This principle will not be discussed here; Rudolf Steiner has gone into it at some length in various places in his work.[32]

However, having identified the second great power with the Muslim world, *TE* writer then studiously ignores religion: 'The driving force was not religion, though that created the movement's sense of identity. It was hyper-nationalism, another region's demand to stride upon the stage.' This of course is Huntington's continentalism or regional nationalism again. We recall that *TE* article of September 1990 had 'Islamistan' as one of the world's regional powers. This Islamistan results from an Islamic military coup in Saudi Arabia by one Colonel Algosaibi in 2011.[33] That other western bugbear and media hate-figure, Gadaffi, is also a Colonel, so the choice of this particular military rank is probably not accidental. Algosaibi apparently succeeds, because 'he quickly took control of almost all the Gulf's oil; because he could point Muslims towards a new geopolitical target; and, above all, because by 2011 Muslims felt that at last they had a chance to work off their ancient resentment against the now-splintered western world.'

A number of interesting points arise here. Firstly, it is evident that by 2011 no serious alternative to oil as a means of energy is posited. If it were, the geopolitical clout of the Middle Eastern oil-producers would rapidly diminish. But what established the oil industries of the Middle East? British and American capital in the twentieth century! And why was oil allowed to replace electricity as the driving force of the motor industry? It may have something to do with the fact that oil as a subterranean form of energy is closely bound up with the land where it is discovered. This means that major Powers seek domination over those areas they wish to control; oil makes this possible, especially if the Powers happen to be advanced techological states.[34] On 9 December 1917 the British took Jerusalem from the Turks, the first time since the First Crusade that a 'Christian' army had marched into that city. A month earlier (9 November 1917) the Balfour Declaration had been made by the British Government to the Zionists' representative in Britain, who just happened to be Baron Rothschild, the head of the Jewish finance house to which the British Government had been deeply indebted since Nathan Rothschild's millions had helped Wellington to defeat Napoleon.[35] The Zionists were promised a permanent homeland in Palestine for Jews. During the Palestine Mandate in the 1920s and 30s, the British maintained, as usual, that they were trying to be even-handed in their dealings with the Zionist settlers and the Palestinian Arabs. But considering the scale of their debt to Jewish financial houses and the fact that serious oil exploration was not yet underway in Arab countries, there was little competition. Effectively, the British prepared the way for a Jewish state in Palestine, and when, after 1945, they were too exhausted to go further, they handed on the Palestine baton to the UN which, as a creation of the Council on Foreign Relations, was totally dominated by the USA. Since the establishment of the State of Israel in 1948 Israel has been *de facto* a client state of the USA, receiving by far the lion's share of US overseas aid without which it could not exist.

It is not too far-fetched to suggest that none of this would have happened if electricity had been allowed to replace the internal combustion engine in the first decades of the century. The oil power of the Arab states is inextricably linked to Anglo-American control of the Middle East, which has enabled America to intervene to 'protect' Israel. The British could have claimed until 1947 that, even without oil, the Middle East was important geopolitically to secure the route to India, but more powerful circles in the USA were determined to bring the old model of territorial and military control over subject peoples — including Britain's Raj — to an end. The more subtle means of economic domination was to be the name of the game in the age of the world economy.

Jerusalem, the site of Christ's Crucifixion and Resurrection, is the spiritual-physical centre of the world, not Greenwich(!), and the ahrimanic powers are determined to control it in preparing for the imminent advent of their own champion — Antichrist. They have used the oil issue as a geopolitical pretext to allow them to interfere in the Middle East, claiming to be upholding the cause of the world economy. There are other aspects, of course, to the oil issue, such as pollution and its effects on society, but the question of control over Jerusalem and Palestine is primary.

Micro-assault on the middle: Turkey

It is significant, therefore, that *TE* writer nowhere in this article mentions Israel, Palestine or Jerusalem as objects of Arab ambition, but rather 'a new geopolitical target', which, two paragraphs later, turns out to be none other than Russia: 'The main target ... was the *decaying corpse of Russia*' [emphasis TMB]. We recall that in the *Truth* map of 1890 Russia was depicted as a 'desert'; a hundred years later it is described as 'a decaying corpse'. The hatred of Russia in the élite circles of the West would seem to know no bounds.

Prior to the assault on Russia, however, the armies of what *TE* calls 'the New Caliphate' (to reinforce the cultural divide by the use of a phrase that harks back to the militant beginnings of Islam and its first attacks on the West) destroy that nation which has in the twentieth century sought to play a bridging role between Europe and Asia, namely, Turkey. This is typical of the tactics of Ahriman. He seeks always to remove the middle term, to assault the central mediating area, the heart and rhythmic system in the human being, in order to bring head and limbs into direct contact with each other. Thus was Central Europe and especially the Germanic cultural region attacked in the twentieth century to create a bipolar Europe, while in the even more global power structure of the twenty-first century it is those countries such as Russia and Turkey, which serve to mediate between cultural regions that are to be attacked.

Huntington too indicates the coming assault on Turkey, calling it 'a torn country':

> In the future, as people differentiate themselves by civilization, countries with large numbers of peoples of different civilizations, such as the Soviet Union [sic] and Yugoslavia, are candidates for dismemberment. Some other countries ... are divided over whether their society

belongs to one civilization or another. These are torn countries. Their leaders typically wish to pursue a bandwagoning strategy and to make their countries members of the West, but the history, culture and traditions of their countries are non-Western. The most obvious and prototypical torn country is Turkey ... Turkey will not become a member of the European Community, and the real reason, as President Ozal said, 'is that we are Muslim and they are Christian and they don't say that'. Having rejected Mecca, and then being rejected by Brussels, where does Turkey look? Tashkent may be the answer. The end of the Soviet Union gives Turkey the opportunity to become the leader of a revived Turkic civilization involving seven countries from the borders of Greece to those of China. *Encouraged by the West* [emphasis TMB], Turkey is making strenuous efforts to carve out this new identity for itself.[36]

This is a fascinating piece of writing. First there is the denial of any true kind of cosmopolitan impulse; peoples are to separate themselves into civilizational (racial writ large) blocs. Then there is the denial of the mediating role played by countries such as Turkey; these are to be pushed back, either in terms of space (territory) or time (historical development) into different civilizational groups away from 'the West'. Having emerged from Central Asia over a thousand years ago and moving west to play a major world-historical role in helping Europe to define itself, the Turks are now to be 'encouraged' to move back, as it were, emotionally if not physically, to Central Asia. Carrots are dangled by Huntington in front of the members of the unsuspecting (?) Turkish élite who may be reading *Foreign Affairs* as he speaks of Turkey as 'the leader', 'a revived Turkic civilization', 'from the borders of Greece to those of China'. We note the magical number 'seven countries'.

Huntington's statements are all illusion-mongering. A look at the map immediately shows that between Turkey and the realization of any such Pan-Turkic dreams lies the Christian state of Armenia and the non-Turkic regional superpower of Iran. To 'encourage' Pan-Turkic dreaming on Turkey's part so that it looks east instead of west to Europe will mean to involve it in endless power struggles with at least those two states and probably also with Georgia and Russia. It would be irresponsible in the extreme. But just as the West encouraged Russia's Pan-Slavic dreaming in the nineteenth century, urging it to become a Piedmont or a Prussia for a union of Europe's Slavs, so the West now seems to be setting up similar illusions for Turkey to chase after, while cruelly preparing for her quite a different fate, as described in *TE* article. The West did the same for Russia, despite being allied to her, from 1894 to 1917.

Returning to *TE*, its scenario has Turkey succumbing to 'the forces of the New Caliphate' in 2014–2016, when, a hundred years after the Gallipoli offensive, the Arab armies sweep 'up to the Bosporus' and establish 'their first bridgehead in south-eastern Europe'. It does not say how far into the Balkans they press, perhaps only as far as the present Turkish frontier, but that vagueness contributes to arousing European anxieties. In a bizarre convolution of the Crimean War and the Suez fiasco of 1956, the British and the French attempt to save Turkey in a vain expedition to Antioch in 2014. Obviously they do not try very hard.

Huntington's article goes on to say that a torn country must meet three criteria in order 'to redefine its civilization identity':

First, its political and economic élite has to be generally supportive and enthusiastic about this move. Second, its public has to be willing to acquiesce in the redefinition.

Third, *the dominant groups* in the recipient civilization [in this case, the West, TMB] have to be willing to embrace the convert [emphasis TMB]. All three requirements in large part exist with respect to Mexico. The first two in large part exist with respect to Turkey.[37]

No doubt Huntington believes that Japan, surely a classic case of a 'torn country', meets these criteria, for he has very little to say about it. In 1993 Mexico was about to be swallowed by the USA in NAFTA, hence its threefold qualification, yet Huntington was not right about the Mexican public's willing acquiescence, for several months after his article a major rebellion against the pro-NAFTA Salinas government broke out in the far south of the country which was only with great difficulty repressed. Japan and Mexico, however, are for the time being destined to 'belong to the West', so they meet the criteria. The 'dominant groups' in the West will not accept Turkey, and so it must turn East.

Macro-assault on the middle: Russia between hammer and anvil

When it comes to Russia's membership of the West, Huntington is unequivocal: 'It is not clear that any of [the three requirements] exist with respect to Russia's joining the West.'[38] Despite all he has said or implied about religious and racial links, Russia is to be permanently barred from the club. He goes on in the following astonishing passage:

The conflict between liberal democracy and Marxism-Leninism was between ideologies which, despite their major differences, ostensibly shared ultimate goals of freedom, equality and prosperity. A traditional, authoritarian, nationalist Russia could have quite different goals. A western democrat could carry on an intellectual debate with a Soviet Marxist. It would be virtually impossible for him to do that with a Russian traditionalist. If, as the Russians stop behaving like Marxists, they reject liberal democracy and begin behaving like Russians but not like westerners, the relations between Russia and the West could again become distant and conflictual.[39]

We note the reference to the ideals of the French Revolution, but with prosperity in place of Fraternity. The Marxism of Karl Marx could arguably be described as looking to freedom, equality and prosperity, if only for the working class, but Marxism-Leninism—never. Huntington casually forgets or ignores the millions who died as a direct result of Lenin's actions and the brutal way in which he crushed the freedom of the individual. Western 'democrats' actually carried on innumerable discussions with Russian traditionalists and nationalists in the years before the Revolution, and frequently despaired of conversations with Soviet Marxists who merely parroted official lines. The Russians, says Huntington, must behave neither like Soviets nor like Russians, but only like us, and then we shall accept them—in other words, never. This is the same argument as that used by George Kennan in his infamous Long Telegram from Moscow of 2 February 1946, which contained the substance of his anonymous 'X' article published in *Foreign Affairs* in July 1947. That caused a sensation and its advocacy of the policy of containment and a bipolar world was adopted by the US as its guiding foreign policy principle. Russia, argued Kennan, must be 'contained' not because it is the Soviet Union but because it is Russia, a culture whose psychology was fundamentally out of sync with that of the West.

If the western democrat could carry on 'an intellectual debate' with the Soviet Marxist it was because they shared an atheistic, materialistic and utilitarian view of life, whereas the Russian traditionalist would maintain that a certain fundamentally religious, and indeed Christian, spiritual power resides within the Russian people, as in fact it does in every people in so far as all peoples are guided by Folk Spirits, or Archangels. It is this spiritual dimension that the 'enlightened democratic materialist' cannot abide. For the same reason, many men of the West have felt uncomfortable with the Romanticism of the Germans, which also points to an inner spiritual world both within the human soul and among people in communities (*das Volk*). The occult brotherhoods lodged primarily in the English-speaking West regard themselves as being at war with those elements within German and Russian culture which point to the spirit for human beings in the fifth and sixth epochs respectively. As a result of their wars against Germany in the twentieth century, they believe they have German culture under their thumb, its spiritualizing jacks firmly nailed down in the bourgeois boxes of the NATO/EU-ensconced Federal Republic. Russia too has been dealt severe blows but such a strong residual power remains within the Russian people that it must be hammered still further if it is to be rendered unfit to play its seminal role in the sixth epoch, so that that epoch may be permanently postponed.

The means to provide that hammer blow Huntington turns to immediately after the passage quoted above, which section began with an analysis of Turkey as a 'torn country'. In *TE* article, it also comes immediately after the description of the attack on Turkey in 2014–16. It is described by Huntington as 'the Confucian-Islamic connection' and in *TE* as 'the Chinese-Muslim alliance'.

Huntington is more vague about this than is *TE*. He declares that 'the Confucian-Islamic connection ... has emerged to challenge western interests, values and power'.[40] The evidence he adduces for this is the weapons and technology sales between East Asia (China and North Korea) and the Middle East. Russia and the West are reducing their military capacity while 'the renegades' of the East are greatly increasing theirs. He mentions weapons and nuclear technology sales from China and North Korea to Libya, Iraq, Pakistan and Syria. 'A Confucian-Islamic military connection has thus come into being, designed to promote acquisition by its members of the weapons and weapon technologies needed to counter the military power of the West.'[41]

TE scenario for the twenty-first century is more forthright than Huntington's 'connection' of the last decades of the twentieth century. Instead of wishing to oppose the West and its main client states in the Middle East, Israel and Egypt, as one might expect it would have done and as Huntington implies, the new Islamic superpower turns against Russia, the country which bridges globally between the West and the East. '... here [in Russia] the New Caliphate found the basis for the alliance with China that was to shape the next two centuries.' That takes us up to the year 2200, in other words, it covers the entire Age of Michael which began in 1879 and which we can assume will continue until at least 2233. At first, it is said, the Chinese and Muslims wanted to take from Russia old territories that had been theirs in the past, but that then 'having achieved that [the new Muslim power] found itself pushing still further north'. A very vague phrase indeed. One wonders whether anyone might have 'encouraged' it to go on pushing further north into lands north of Kazakhstan and east of the Urals which were never Muslim territory.

'China supplied most of the weapons the Caliphate needed. The Caliphate provided China with a secure western flank.' The weapons issue we saw in Huntington; we can assume that the vast quantities of sophisticated weapons needed would have come from the huge and sophisticated Chinese arms industry and economy that had developed as a result of *western* and overseas Chinese investment. The mention of the secure western flank seems totally bogus, and again ignores the religious question, since many of the peoples living in the westernmost areas of China are Muslim minorities. The Caliphate would be a less comfortable neighbour than the Russians, who have never shown any interest in invading that part of China.[42]

'By the mid-twenty-first century, all this had been accomplished...' Apparently, the Russians 'did not use their decrepit nuclear weapons for fear of an overwhelming Chinese response'. In other words, the rest of the world, and notably 'the West', did nothing while China built up a nuclear attack capability greater than that of Russia. And why perhaps? Maybe because the West was so concerned — as it has been since Manchester mill-owners first drooled over the possibilities of selling cotton to China in the decades before the First Opium War — with getting into the world's most populous market. By the year 2050 then, 'in two brief campaigns Russia's borders were pushed back to the Urals and to an uneasy line running from the central Urals to the Sea of Azov'. This would reduce Russia to something like the size it was at the time of Ivan the Terrible in the mid-sixteenth century! This is the kind of emasculation which élite forces in the West would like to see Russia suffer.

The second of the article's three illustrations (see p.145) is divided in two by what looks like the Great Wall of China. Below it is desert-like country with three oil wells each flying a crescent flag. A huge dragon has advanced from that country across the wall into the seemingly lusher, more forested land north of the wall where a bear (much smaller than the dragon) is trying to ward off the dragon's flames. The China-Muslim alliance is thus represented by an unpleasant-looking, snakelike dragon and Russia by a more friendly-looking bear standing on its hind legs in a more human fashion. The racialist allusions are obvious.

RUSSIA, 1533 — 1598

MAP 13

Russia c. 1584 at the death of Ivan the Terrible

Despite their supposed 'ancient resentment' against the West, however, the Muslims will not attack Europe, because, 'knowing that the Europeans still had a powerful nuclear force [the alliance] cautiously decided to push its expansion no further'. How convenient for Europe! Once again, as in the disastrous fourteenth century, Europe is effectively saved from a hammering at the hands of the eastern hordes. And again Russia is destroyed instead, while the West, as in the fourteenth century, merely looks on. To spare the racial vanity of *TE* readers perhaps, Western Europe cannot be seen to surrender to the Chinese-Muslim alliance. *TE* writer knows this, because, despite his talk of American hemispheric isolationism in the twenty-first century, he knows that in fact plans are afoot to effect a union between America and Western Europe via

the TAFTA project (*TE* article of September 1990 was the first public revelation of this in the UK).

The ultimate triumph of the West's 'great ideas': the end of history revisited

Having described the destruction of Russia by the Confucian-Islamic alliance, the article then moves towards its conclusion, and a very vague conclusion it is. The reason why the democracies missed their opportunity in the 1990s is said to have been because they failed 'to examine the ideas that had created' the cycle of history that was coming to an end. That cycle had seen the triumph of the Age of Rationality over the Age of Faith, 'the rights and responsibilities of the individual began to be asserted against the spirit of authority'. It had begun with 'the pair of events known as the Renaissance and the Reformation'. Indeed this spirit of individuality had a lot to do with the Reformation and with Christianity, but as usual, the latter is nowhere credited by *TE*. The stress on the Renaissance and the Reformation, as well as the Enlightenment, but again without including the Christian dimension, also featured heavily in *TE* article of September 1990. These were described as having 'produced the European-American culture that shaped the next half-millennium', by which the writer no doubt has predominantly in mind Britain and America, the English-speaking world rather than, say, German-speaking culture.

By his admonition to 're-examine the ideas that had created this cycle', the writer may well have had efforts in mind such as Francis Fukuyama's 1992 book *The End of History, and the Last Man*, a paean of praise to the Anglo-Saxon values of the late eighteenth century which informed the founding of the USA. In his book Fukuyama cleverly twists the ideas of a German thinker, Hegel, as manipulated in their turn by the Franco-Russian academic Alexandre Kojève,[43] and uses them as the basic concepts of a work which claims that humanity cannot really improve on Anglo-Saxon notions of liberal democracy and the market economy, and that the future will consist merely of tinkerings and adjustments to this system. Fukuyama admits that 'experience suggests that if men cannot struggle on behalf of a just cause because that just cause was victorious in an earlier generation, then they will struggle against that just cause. They will struggle for the sake of struggle ... out of a certain boredom ... And if the greater part of the world in which they live is characterized by peaceful and prosperous liberal democracy, then they will struggle against that peace and prosperity, and against democracy.'[44]

He goes on:

We who live in the old age of mankind might come to the following conclusion. No ... 'socio-economic system' is able to satisfy all men in all places . . . dissatisfaction arises precisely where democracy has triumphed most completely . . . those who remain dissatisfied will always have the potential to restart history. Moreover it appears to be the case that rational recognition is not self-sustaining, but must rely on pre-modern, non-universal forms of recognition to function properly. Stable democracy requires a sometimes irrational democratic culture, and a spontaneous civil society growing out of pre-liberal traditions. Capitalist prosperity is best promoted by a strong work ethic, which in turn depends on the ghosts of dead religious beliefs, if not those beliefs themselves, or else an irrational commitment to nation or race.'[45]

Here Fukuyama is, perhaps unwittingly, pointing to the way in which the media in western democratic countries manipulate the more atavistic elements in those societies to gain the support of the masses for the countries' élites. The British Empire, for example, was commonly declared in Britain to be a universal good spreading civilization throughout the globe, and yet Britons were at the same time exhorted to keep their distance from 'the inferior races' they were supposed to be helping. More recently, Americans were constantly being told their Vietnam War was to spread the benefits of civilization, freedom and democracy to the peoples of Asia, yet their popular entertainment, in films ranging from *The Green Berets* to *Rambo* frequently portrayed Asians as subhumans whose lives could be snuffed out at will and *en masse*. In much of the debate surrounding EU membership in Britain today we can see the same appeals to a crude atavism being made by media people who in the next breath boast of the moral superiority of Britain and America.

However, Fukuyama does not believe that the irrational rebels within the bosom of bourgeois liberal democracy will ultimately overthrow it, because, he argues, the horrors of the twentieth century have shown what happens when liberal democracy is challenged, and secondly, because 'standing as a bulwark against the revival of history and the return of the first man is the imposing Mechanism [note the capital letter! — TMB] of modern science ... the Mechanism driven by unlimited desire and guided by reason'.[46] Fukuyama then leads to a conclusion of brilliant ambiguity:

> If it is true that the historical process rests on the twin pillars of rational desire and rational recognition [might this perhaps be an allusion to the twin pillars of Masonic lodges, Jachin and Boaz? — TMB] and that liberal democracy is the best political system that best satisfies the two in some kind of balance, then it would seem that the chief threat to democracy would be our own confusion about what is really at stake. For while modern societies have evolved towards democracy, modern thought has arrived at an impasse [one which Fukuyama's entire book seeks to justify, a literal dead-end of history portrayed as a kind of socio-political nirvana! — TMB], unable to come to a consensus on what constitutes man and his specific dignity, and consequently unable to define the rights of man ... This confusion in thought can occur despite the fact that history is being driven in a coherent direction by rational desire and rational recognition, and despite the fact that liberal democracy constitutes the best possible solution to the human problem.[47]

Cultural relativism, he says, will give way before 'the homogenization of mankind ... as a result of economic development',[48] by which, of course, both he and *TE* understand homogenization to mean Anglo-Saxonization.

Fukuyama closes his book with a coda, a metaphor of humanity arriving at the promised homogenized land, which turns out to be — California! 'Rather than a thousand shoots blossoming into as many different flowering plants, mankind will come to seem like a long wagon train strung out along a road.'[49] In his extended, rather laboured metaphor, which could hardly be more American, he sees the majority of the wagons pulling into town: 'Enough wagons would pull into town such that any reasonable person looking at the situation would be forced to agree that there had only been one journey and one destination.'[50] Some, of course, would not make it: 'Several wagons, attacked by Indians, will have been set aflame and abandoned along the way.'[51] By Indians, he perhaps had the Confucian-Islamic alliance attacking Russia in mind here. 'Others will have found alternative routes to the main road, though they will discover that to get through the final mountain range they all must use the same pass.'[52] (Many Japanese readers of his book may shift uncomfortably here.) The book's last sentence is a masterpiece of ambiguity: 'Nor can we in the final analysis know, provided a majority of the wagons eventually reach the same town, whether their occupants, having looked around a bit at their new surroundings, will not find them inadequate and set their eyes on a new and more distant journey.'[53] To new socio-political arrangements on another planet perhaps, abandoning earth? Having arrived in California, where else can man go but up? This sentence would seem to contradict his argument, but it merely serves to cloak it with an air of balance and open-mindedness; in fact, the whole book has been leading up to the triumphal wagon train across America.

From Fukuyama's Wild West coda we pass over to the interesting little coda at the end of TE article, which is headed 'The end of the cycle'. Here, too, we see a cloak of balance and apparent open-mindedness. The Age of Reason went too far; it led to the French and the Russian Revolutions which 'did irrational things in the name of reason'. The fact that British-inspired materialist philosophy and natural science were the main driving forces behind these revolutions is of course nowhere mentioned.[54] The errors are attributed only to non-Anglo-Saxons: the French, the Russians and the 'Fascist upheavals of the 1920s and 1930s' (23 thus puts in a penultimate appearance), i.e. the Germans, the Italians and the Spanish. 'Nationalism and its son hypernationalism, were milder versions of the same reaction.' Again, the racism that informed much of Britain's imperial drives, not to mention *TE*'s own advocacy of continental or civilizational hypernationalism in its September 1990 article, are left unmentioned. Irrationality in socio-political life is not to be associated with the English-speaking world; it is something that only foreigners indulge in.

Then comes the cloak, an extremely vague sop to the spirit of the 1990s, to the Green or New Age consciousness:

A new balance was needed between the analytic part of the human mind and the instinctive part, between rationality and feeling ... a new bargain had to be struck between the claims of individual freedom and the claims of a universal morality; only then could law and liberty swing evenly on the scales. Because they did not tackle these problems in time, the democracies marched straight from the climax of their twentieth-century victory into an anticlimax. They did not know what to do next.

Apart from the interesting references to Libran images of balance and scales, this proffered 'solution' to the problems of the 1990s, one small paragraph in a three-page article, is so vague it offers no concrete and constructive proposals to stand alongside the extremely concrete and destructive scenario it lays out for the coming half-century. In its seeming generosity of spirit, and its actual paucity and vagueness it resembles the last three sentences of Huntington's article, in which, after 27 pages of almost constant *realpolitik* focusing both implicitly and explicitly on the power interests of 'the West', Huntington disingenuously declares that the West will need 'to develop a more profound understanding of the basic religious and philosophical assumptions underlying other civilizations and the ways in which people in those civilizations see their interests. It will require an effort to identify elements of commonality between western and other civilizations.'[55] This is as far as Huntington goes away from the direction of pure power politics.

The 'democracies' (read Britain and America) however, or rather those élite circles who seek to manipulate them, know only too well what to do next. *TE* in September 1990, in December 1992, and in May 1995 (as well as *Foreign Affairs*, notably in Huntington's article) have indicated what their intentions are.

The five sentences of the final paragraph point to the apotheosis of their plans in the distant thirtieth century. The fateful number 23 makes its last implicit appearance in the first two sentences: 'It is easy in 2992 to say this. Today's 3 billion people...' $2 + 9 + 9 + 2 = 22$. The population in the thirtieth century is stated to be 3 billion people. Today it is 6 billion. In other words, the world's population will have to lose 3 billion people between now and then! Since the article is concerned only with events in the twenty-first century, at most up to the twenty-third century (the end of the Arch-angelic Regency of Michael), and not at all with the twenty-third–thirtieth centuries, we may presume that the 3 billion are to disappear before the end of the Michaelic Age and possibly even during the twenty-first century — a holocaust by which the twentieth century will pale in comparison.

The necessary 'rebalancing' of rationality and feeling mentioned in the penultimate paragraph has apparently been achieved only by the thirtieth century, and then 'only in part'. But the rebalancing mentioned is hardly of a cultural or spiritual nature; it is entirely geopolitical. The rebalancings 'have seen China and the Muslims move into their own new period of division and uncertainty; Russia reassemble itself; America come back into the world: and Europe settle for prosy but workable reality. The conditions of a *Pax Democratica* have at last arrived.' It has thus taken some 900 years for the Chinese and the Muslims to falter and fail! This is hardly conceivable. Russia will 'reassemble itself', but on what basis is hinted at in the preamble below the title to the article: 'Dwight Bogdanov and Vladimir Lowell (University of California in Moscow)', i.e. a Russia under American cultural control. America will 'come back into the world', whereas in fact America will continue to control the world all through any period of neo-isolationism, just as it did in the 1920s by manipulation of the world economy. Most dismissively of all, Europe, which is seen as an old has-been, will 'settle for prosy but workable reality'. This is the ultimate snub for any cultural and spiritual pretensions which either the Catholic-Latin countries or the German-speaking and Nordic countries may have. Europe is to be solidly bourgeois and materialist—nothing else. It is to stay in its place, obeying the will of its English-speaking masters; for it is they, and not the Vatican's dreams of a renewed Carolingian superstate, who are creating the conditions for the emergence of the new Roman Empire of our time.

After *Pax Romana* came *Pax Britannica* in the nineteenth century, ruled by a class who consciously modelled themselves after Roman examples. They handed on the imperial baton to their equally race-conscious cousins over the water and we had *Pax* (!) *Americana* in the twentieth century. *TE* does not wish to say that the twenty-first century or even the thirtieth century will also be the age of *Pax Americana*—that would be, well, indiscreet. So, instead, it speaks of *Pax Democratica*, but what it means is *Pax Anglica*—the continued domination of the world by the Anglo-American, English-speaking élites, the senators of the New Roman World Empire. For in this crucial fifth post-Atlantean epoch, in this epoch that has seen the onset of the Second

Coming of Christ, it is the destiny of America to play the role of Rome, the tempter of humanity.

Pax Democratica signifies the end of history as meant by Fukuyama and his intellectual mentor Kojève, the end of human evolution, frozen at the stage of the fifth epoch. Kojève wrote:

> The disappearance of man at the end of History ... is not a cosmic catastrophe: the natural world remains what it has been from all eternity. And therefore it is not a biological catastrophe either: man remains alive as animal in harmony with nature or given Being. What disappears is man properly so-called—that is, Action negating the given, and Error, or in general, the Subject opposed to the Object...[56]

Commenting on this, Fukuyama wrote:

> [Men] would satisfy their needs through economic activity, but they would no longer have to risk their lives in battle. They would, in other words, become animals again, as they were before the bloody battle that began history ... [Kojève] indicated that the end of history meant also the end of both art and philosophy ... there would be no eras and no particular distinction of the human spirit for artists to portray.

Quoting Kojève again, he added: 'What would disappear ... is not only philosophy or the search for discursive Wisdom, but also that Wisdom itself. For in these post-historical animals, there would no longer be any [discursive] understanding of the World and of self.'[57]

Ultimately, what Fukuyama and *TE* are proposing for the near future of humanity is not so much any kind of nationalistic Anglo-American domination; it is the enslavement of the human spirit and its subjection to a single pattern of life, its recognition of only one God, Mammon, or Antichrist, who in this epoch is working to achieve his purposes not exclusively but pre-eminently through a new World Empire that is to be for the fifth epoch what Rome was on a smaller scale for the fourth epoch. America and the English-speaking world have been and are still to be the intended prime instruments for the establishment of this Empire.[58]

In the early nineteenth century that prescient observer of American society, the Frenchman Alexis de Tocqueville, foresaw a new kind of slavery arising out of radical individualism in the brave new world of the United States. Today, his vision seems about to become concrete:

> I seek to trace the novel features under which despotism may appear in the world. The first thing that strikes the observation is an innumerable multitude of men, all equal and alike, incessantly endeavouring to procure the petty and paltry pleasures with which they glut their lives. Each of them, living apart, is as a stranger to the fate of all the rest; his children and his private friends constitute to him the whole of mankind. As for the rest of his fellow citizens, he is close to them, but does not see them; he touches them, but he does not feel them; he exists only in himself and for himself alone; and if his kindred still remain to him, he may be said at any rate to have lost his country.
>
> Above this race of men stands an immense and tutelary power, which takes upon itself alone to secure their gratifications and to watch over their fate. That power is absolute, minute, regular, provident, and mild. It would be like the authority of a parent if, like that authority, its object was to prepare men for manhood; but it seeks, on the contary, to keep them in perpetual childhood; it is well content that the people should rejoice, provided they think of nothing but rejoicing.[59]

Conclusion

Many Americans, but few Britons, are alert to the occult aims and methods of those sections of the Anglo-American élite that serve Ahriman. Most of the alert ones, the rational as well as the irrational, belong to isolated libertarian groups, far right Christian fundamentalist groups or violent militia organizations. As such they are easily marginalized by the media, and the clandestine purposes of the élites whom many in the media serve are not seen through. Ahriman works through lies, half-truths and deceptions; above all he wishes not to be seen as he works. Once light is thrown upon his works, like a spider he shrivels and scampers away. Spiders are part of the natural order; they have their place and function. They are neither to be feared nor hated, but they must be *understood* so that one does not blunder blindly into their webs. The most far-reaching secrets are not seen precisely because they are placed in the open, where they are overlooked among the mass of information that is available in today's world. Such is the nature of the writings that have been considered and analysed in this book. It is to be hoped that in the months and years to come more and more people in the English-speaking world will awake to the sinister plans being made for their future by powerful élite forces which serve Ahriman and which wear media masks. If this book can contribute in any way to the exposure of those plans, it will have served its purpose.

Postscript

The seventy-fifth anniversary number of *Foreign Affairs* (Sept/Oct 1997, Vol. 76, No. 5) carried a major article by Zbigniew Brzezinski entitled 'A Geostrategy for Eurasia'. The article was adapted from Brzezinski's soon-to-be-published book *The Grand Chessboard*. In his article Brzezinski lays bare some of the broad strategic thinking current in CFR élite circles about the direction the world ought to go in the twenty-first century if 'America's global primacy and historical legacy' is to be maintained — a primacy which Brzezinski of course considers to be vital for world progress. The main challengers to this primacy he sees in Eurasia. He describes a short-term scenario (5 years), maintaining 'the prevailing geopolitical pluralism on the map of Eurasia; a medium-term scenario (5–20 years), a trans-Eurasian security system formed by 'strategically compatible' countries 'prompted by American leadership'; and a long-term scenario (20 + years), a 'genuinely shared (global) political leadership'. America is seen as the world's 'indispensable nation' in terms of its monopoly on power, defined in four dimensions: military, economic, technological, and cultural.

'A benign American hegemony' must ensure a) that Russia remains 'post-imperial' and closely tied to Western Europe, i.e. responsive to US influence in Europe. It is noteworthy, however, that nothing is said about Russia being allowed to join the EU. In the section devoted to Russia, which is entitled 'Russia's Historic Task', nothing is said about this task other than Russia should 'make its long-delayed post-imperial decision in favour of Europe'. Earlier in this book, however, we have considered that Russia's true historic task is to act as mediator between Europe and Asia, so that it might best prepare for its work of fostering a spiritualization of the feeling life and of true brotherhood and community in the sixth post-Atlantean epoch. If it is to fulfil this role, Russia cannot be under the thumb of the United States, especially in the cultural-spiritual realm. Brzezinski, however, wishes to pull Russia over into the West completely by confederating and decentralizing it. First, the old USSR territories were transformed into the Commonwealth of Independent States (CIS) after 1991. Now he wishes to go further and break up Russia itself, so that Russia east of the Urals may be decoupled from European Russia. His intention is that Russia will thus return essentially to its medieval boundaries, as was discussed in Chapter 3 of this book.

His article includes a map which shows a threefold division of a confederated Russia: Russia proper, Siberia, and the Far Eastern republic of Eastern Siberia. These states

Eurasia in the twenty-first century according to Zbigniew Brezezinski, from Foreign Affairs, *Sept/Oct 1997, Vol. 76, No. 5*

'would find it easier', he claims, 'to cultivate closer economic ties with [their] neighbours—i.e. such sparsely populated states would find it easier to be bullied and effectively, if not overtly, taken over by their far more populous Muslim and Chinese neighbours to the south and east. A 'decentralized political system and free-market economics,' he says, 'would be most likely to unleash the creative potential of the Russian people and Russia's vast natural resources.' On the contrary, these are precisely the socio-economic features that run counter to the Russian folk-temperament and would act as a poison to its constitution, as western-style free market economics, in particular, is already doing.

Brzezinski lays emphasis on the need to safeguard the sovereignty of the new post-Soviet states and focuses on Ukraine (which has a divided Catholic and Orthodox population) and, in Central Asia, on Uzbekistan. We recall *The Economist*'s mysterious 'new Muslim entity' and the likelihood that this might emerge precisely from Uzbekistan, in which Washington seems to be particularly interested. The Ukraine, which Brzezinski insists must be 'identified as a Central European country' (!), will be allowed to join NATO and the EU, while Russia will not. The western boundary of Brzezinski's 'Atlanticist [i.e. US-dominated] Europe' runs in his map along the eastern borders of the Ukraine, Belarus, the Baltic states and Finland. South of Russia, large-scale international investment in Central Asia would prop up the new states and benefit Russia, while boosting prosperity all round, providing stability, and helping to avoid 'Balkan-type conflicts'. We remember that such investment in the Balkans pre-1914 did nothing to stop the Great War igniting precisely in that region; on the contrary, great power economic rivalry in the region added to it. A twenty-first-century 'great game' over Central Asian oil is already being played out, fuelled by western and Chinese investment.

In Europe itself, Brzezinski argues that the US should work closely with France and Germany if 'Europe is to remain part of the "Euro-Atlantic" space'. Oblivious to proconsul Blair's assertions about Britain's central role in Europe, Britain is nowhere mentioned by Brzezinski, the mouthpiece of CFR-Rockefeller interests; this omission speaks volumes. It surely signifies that for America's East Coast CFR Establishment, Britain is already part of America! The old mother country has been colonized by its offspring. As we have seen, Washington has long regarded France and Germany, especially the former, to be its prime agents in the work of creating a United States of Europe. As a reward to France and a sop to its yearning for overseas influence and *gloire*, Brzezinski says that America must 'eventually' show more 'acceptance of France's concerns over a European role in Africa and the Middle East'. What this means, of course, is that the French wish their old colonial influence in those regions to continue.

America must, says Brzezinski, strive to avoid conflict with the Islamic world and with China. We recall that *The Economist* saw just these two powers as those that, together, would make war on Russia. It is clear, however, that Brzezinski does not expect China to survive as a unified power. It may be powerful militarily, he says, but will remain poor—just as the USSR did. Nevertheless, a sop will also be given to China to satisfy what is perceived to be its age-old desire for regional hegemony. His map shows a 'Greater China' that includes Mongolia, Indo-China, half of Indonesia, Nepal, Pakistan, Afghanistan, and over half of the Central Asian region—in short, a reaffirmation of the old imperial Chinese sphere of influence—with additions. This will keep the Chinese happy, he thinks, and in veiled language he says that China 'might also project *more overt influence* [emphasis—TMB] into the Russian Far East'. His map makes clear that, unlike *The Economist* scenario of late 1992, Japan will not be part of China's sphere of influence; rather it will be firmly under the US thumb. It will not, he says, be America's 'offshore Asian ally against China', although in fact, since at least the Korean War (1950–53), that is exactly what it has been. Rather, 'cooperating closely with the United States' Japan should concentrate on noble and lofty ideal-istic 'global concerns pertaining to developing and peace-keeping'—a 'politically satisfying [and] economically beneficial' 'global vocation'. (Anglo-American statesmen have been particularly fond of such high-flown, seemingly idealistic, yet utterly hypocritical language when they wish to mask their drives for naked power—not for them the 'forthright honesty' of Bismarckian *realpolitik*.) To bring this noble vocation about, Japan and America, says Brze-zinski, should create a Pacific free trade area to comple-ment the Atlantic free trade area which, he says earlier, America and a united Europe will have established.

America's finger will thus be in every global pie, stirring, directing, and this will be for everyone's benefit under the benign hegemony of the New Roman Empire. The grand design will culminate in a 'trans-Eurasian security system' overseen by a new Security Council consisting of 'America, Europe, China, Japan, a confederated Russia, and India'. This will be 'the major architectural [might it be going too far to say 'freemasonic'?—TMB] initiative of the next century'. It will 'gradually relieve America of some of its burdens' of empire (*pace* Kipling) yet will also 'perpetuate beyond a generation' America's 'decisive role as Eurasia's arbitrator'.

Notes

GA = *Gesamtausgabe*, collected works of Rudolf Steiner in the original German.

Notes to Introduction (pages 1–20)

1. See, for example, *Occult Science – An Outline*, Rudolf Steiner Press, Chapter 4.
2. Steiner also indicated the emergence in our time of a third principle of evil, even more challenging to humanity than Lucifer or Ahriman. He gave it the ancient Persian name of the Asuras. While Lucifer seeks to tempt the ego away from the earth in personal spiritual fantasies, and Ahriman wishes to bind it to the earth and enslave it in a vast machine-like collective, the Asuras simply aim to destroy the human ego, or individuality altogether. While they have begun to act in modern industrial civilization, their time lies far in the future. Until the end of the current physical cycle of Earth's development, Ahriman will continue to be man's chief adversary. See Steiner's lectures of 22 March 1909 (*The Deed of Christ and the Opposing Spiritual Powers*, Steiner Book Centre 1976) and 15 December 1919 (*Ideas for a New Europe*, Rudolf Steiner Press, 1992).
3. See Note 1 and Steiner's lectures on the four Gospels, given 1908–12, published by Rudolf Steiner Press and Anthroposophic Press.
4. See *The Influences of Lucifer and Ahriman*, five lectures given in November 1919, Anthroposophic Press 1993.
5. *The Occult Movement in the 19th Century*, Rudolf Steiner Press 1973.
6. Lecture of 4 December 1916, *The Karma of Untruthfulness*, Vol. 1, Rudolf Steiner Press 1988.
7. See C.G. Harrison, *The Transcendental Universe*, Temple Lodge 1993, especially pp. 98–99. Harrison later wrote two further books, *The Creed for the Twentieth Century* (1923), on the rele-

vance of the Nicene Creed, and *The Fourth Mystery* (1929), on birth, death and resurrection.

8. *The Anglo-American Establishment*, written 1949, published 1981, Books In Focus, New York. *Tragedy and Hope*, Macmillan, New York 1966.
9. Ibid. p. xi.
10. Ibid., p. 197.
11. Ibid.

Notes to Chapter 1 (pages 21–49)

1. It is necessary straight away to point out a significant error or, possibly, a misinterpretation that has unfortunately been repeated in the English translation of lectures by Rudolf Steiner given in 1916/17, entitled *The Karma of Untruthfulness*, Vol. I, lecture 1, for the reader will immediately notice that whereas on p.289 (Note 6) of that translation it states '...Where Russia would be is written "Russian Desert." Countries for Socialist experiments', the phrase 'Countries for Socialist experiments' does not in fact appear on the map. The original German has: 'Über dem Raum Russland steht das Wort "desert" (Wüste) = Staaten für sozialistische Experimente.' Note that Polzer-Hoditz uses the word 'Wort' (word) not 'Wörter' (words), and the words 'Staaten für sozialistische Experimente' are not enclosed in quotation marks as is the word 'desert', which does actually appear on the map. It is possible that Polzer-Hoditz himself was under the misapprehension that the phrase 'countries for Socialist experiments' was also actually included on the map. This may be because he had heard from his brother during the War that Russia was indeed intended by the western brotherhoods to become a laboratory for social experiments, and, when he wrote his book *Kaiser Karl* (published 1928), had unconsciously allowed this memory to run into his memory of Labouchère's map. Alternatively, it could be that he did not mean to suggest that the words actually appeared on the map, but rather, by using the = sign, intended simply to characterize the nature of the 'desert' with words whose meaning he may well have understood from Rudolf Steiner,

in which case, the absence of the = sign in the English translation is misleading.

2. The Labour Government's plans for referenda (1997) leading to devolution for Scotland and Wales, which many believe will be the stepping-stones for full independence for Scotland if not Wales and the dissolution of the United Kingdom, will help to realize the late nineteenth-century republican aims of Labouchère and other Radicals. A great filip to the cause of Scottish nationalism was given by the film *Braveheart* (1995) about the medieval Scots hero William Wallace, which could not have been made without Hollywood's help. *The Economist* (22 October 1994) carried a leading article entitled 'An idea whose time has passed' which advocated the end of the monarchy. The significance of this was that the same magazine included a feature titled 'Bagehot', a regular column about British affairs. It was named after Walter Bagehot, the great editor of *The Economist*, contemporary of Henry Labouchère, and constitutional expert whose thoughts on the British monarchy did much to define and bolster the role of the monarchy. The article and the leader implied that *The Economist*, which had defined and upheld the monarchy in the late nineteenth century, was now declaring it defunct. See Chapter 3 for discussion of the position of *The Economist* in the British media hierarchy.

3. See Chapter 3 for discussion of key position of Turkey in the western brotherhoods' plans at the end of the 1990s.

4. *Anthroposophy Today*, No. 11, Autumn 1990, p.37.

5. *The Karma of Untruthfulness* (hereafter KOU), Vol. 1, RSP 1988, lecture 7, 18 December 1916, p.152.

6. KOU.

7. J. Hamill, *The Craft – A History of English Freemasonry*, Crucible 1986.

8. See Renate Riemeck, *Mitteleuropa – Bilanz eines Jahrhunderts* (Central Europe – A Century in the Balance), Fischer Verlag, Frankfurt 1983, Chapters 1 and 2. In brief, Riemeck describes how the Prince's circle, through the Catholic aristocrat the Duke of Norfolk, put a certain picture of the future development of the twentieth century across to both the French and the Vatican. Pope Leo XIII then began to take steps to

bring France and Russia closer. These continued to the point where France was able to make a formal approach to Russia. What the Vatican hoped to achieve from such developments was the ultimate demise of Protestantism in Germany and of Orthodoxy in Russia.

9. Fischer Taschenbuch Verlag, Frankfurt, 1983 (see Note 8).

10. *Mitteleuropa*, p.18.

11. Unlike his grandfather George VI, who was an enthusiastic Freemason, and all previous Princes of Wales reaching back to Frederick Lewis in 1737, Charles has avoided Freemasonry. The Duke of Edinburgh did not wish to become one, but was pressured to do so by his father-in-law, and has since taken a very minimal role in Freemasonry. There are those who have speculated that Charles's refusal to enter the ranks of Britain's premier traditional secret society has not a little to do with the hostility with which he has been treated by sections of the media, notably since his well-publicized remarks about modern architecture and the professionals responsible for some of it. Architecture has traditionally been known as 'the royal art' and is the one at the centre of Freemasonic ritual.

12. KOU, lecture 2, p.38. See also Note 10. Steiner often pointed to the long-running struggle behind the veil of outer events that was waged between Freemasons and Jesuits. Ultimately, this struggle has its roots in two primordial streams of human culture going back to the priestly stream of Abel and the man-of-action stream of Cain. In the Christian era it has manifested in the efforts of the Church to stamp out movements deemed to be heretical: the Gnostics, Manichaeans, Cathars, and Knights Templar. Out of the demise of the last of these in the fourteenth century developed esoteric Freemasonry in early seventeenth-century Scotland. This was injected into English society by James I (1603-25). After English Freemasonry opted to become somewhat more visible with the establishment of a nationwide coordinating organization, Grand Lodge, in London in 1717, it rapidly aligned itself with the interests of the English Establishment, Whig, Protestant and Hanoverian. Freemasonry having quickly spread from England to the Continent where it invariably attracted men of 'enlightened' views dangerous to

the Catholic establishments there, Freemasons were declared excommunicate by the Pope in 1738 and Catholics forbidden to associate with them or to join the Craft. Since then, the Society of Jesus, the standard-bearers of the Counter-Reformation, has carried on an unremitting struggle against Freemasonry.

13. It needs to be emphasized that it is not claimed here that all Freemasons are willing tools of higher powers serving ends inimical to human progress. Most Freemasons are completely unaware even of the real meaning of the symbols of their own rituals (a point made by Rudolf Steiner several times and also by the authors, both Freemasons, of the recent much-publicized books *The Hiram Key* and *The Second Messiah*) let alone of the occult intentions of some of the higher grade members of their institutions. The same could be said of the Jesuits. See C. Knight and R. Lomas, *The Hiram Key*, Century 1996, and *The Second Messiah*, Century 1997, especially the latter, Chapter 3, where the possibility of 'a great secret' hidden from the membership by the upper echelons is considered and affirmed. The authors also quote from a *Freemason's Quarterly* of 1813 in which 'leading Masonic writers from other traditions warned of the dangers' inherent in the Duke of Kent and the Duke of Sussex's plans to reunite the Freemasonic world which had been split into two camps since 1751: 'Neither the English writer nor the English reader can keep clear from the egotistical insular tendency to look upon England as the central point of the whole system of events in this wide world.' This comes close to the nub of the matters discussed in the present book, for Rudolf Steiner indicated that it is the self-interest and egotism of the English-speaking peoples, i.e. to the luciferic element working within their souls ('our nation is the best!'), to which the occult directors of the secret brotherhoods appeal in order to carry out their intentions, which are of an ahrimanic nature and not at all nationalist in any sense. Ahriman is interested in spreading a super-materialism all over the world. He simply uses certain cultural and national characteristics to facilitate his work. See R. Steiner, lecture of 15 January 1917, GA 174 (*The Karma of Untruthfulness*, Vol II, RSP).

14. See, A.C. Sutton, *Wall Street and the Bolshevik Revolution*, New Rochelle 1974.
15. Lecture VIII, 2 November 1918, Dornach, in *From Symptom to Reality in Modern History*, RSP 1976.
16. D.J. Goodspeed, *The German Wars 1914–1945*, Orbis, London 1978, p.23.
17. See *Mitteleuropa*, Chapter 2, for the details of how the Vatican played its part.
18. See *Time* magazine, 24 February 1992, for a fascinating article ('The Holy Alliance') on how the Vatican and the White House joined forces in 1982 in a covert operation to aid Solidarity and 'hasten the demise of Communism'.
19. *Anthroposophy Today*, No. 11, 1990, p.39. The idea of the 'threefold ordering of society' was Rudolf Steiner's major contribution to socio-economic affairs. He began speaking about it in 1917 as a response to what he considered to be anti-social impulses threatening Europe from the West (President Woodrow Wilson's Fourteen Points) and from the East (Bolshevism). The peoples of Central Europe failed to take up Steiner's initiative. As a result, Europe had nothing to bring against the ideas of East and West and was thus subjected to them: the Cold War began in 1917 and Europe was dominated by America and Russia for most of the century. Steiner asserted that the 'threefolding of society' was an impulse that lay unconsciously within the will of modern humanity. By this he meant the three main areas of social activity — the cultural/spiritual sphere, the legal/political or 'rights' sphere, and the economic sphere — had in the course of human development been seeking to become independent from each other. They had originally been subsumed in the religious sphere; all social activity in ancient Egypt, for example, was rooted in divine commands and archetypes. In the Middle Ages the political sphere emancipated itself gradually from the religious and, since the Renaissance, the economic sphere has been trying to emancipate itself from the political. The eighteenth-century call for 'Liberty, Equality, and Fraternity' reflected this, but European society has since failed to realize the promise of that call in practical social arrangements. The three spheres must be allowed their own

areas of free activity while at the same time relating to the other areas. Endless social problems today result from the confusion and co-mingling of the three realms: under Communism, politics dominates the other two realms; Anglo-American capitalism makes economic imperatives dominant. Steiner's ideas on the threefolding of society were grounded in his spiritual understanding of the human being as a threefold organism which mirrors the threefold ordering of the spiritual world itself with its nine levels of consciousness organized in three groups. See his books *Towards Social Renewal* and *The Riddles of the Soul* for further details.

20. See for example his lecture of 7 January 1915, Berlin, included in *The Destinies of Individuals and of Nations*, RSP 1986; see also S.O. Prokofieff, 'The Future of the Slavic Peoples of the East and the Spiritual Tasks of Central Europe', *Golden Blade*, 1991, for a comprehensive discussion of this question.

21. W.J. Stein *The British – Their Psychology and Destiny*, Temple Lodge 1990.

22. R. Steiner, lecture of 25 November 1917.

23. See Note 20. It was during the reign of James I (1603–25) that Freemasonry entered the English Establishment from Scotland; also the seeds of British control of North America and India were laid, Britain became Great Britain, the Authorized Version of the Bible was created, and Britain reached out to intervene in the affairs of both Russia and Japan and played a decisive part (precisely by its deliberate inaction) in the course of the Thirty Years War and the failure of the Rosicrucian movement on the Continent. Steiner referred to a personality incarnated 'at the end of the sixteenth century and the beginning of the seventeenth ... in a British body in which there was in truth only little British blood, but more a combination of French and Scottish...' 'From this soul,' said Steiner there proceeded that which gave the impulses to the external as well as to the occult-spiritual life of Britain.' (Lecture of 28 March 1916, GA 167.) This oblique reference is surely to James I. Elsewhere, Steiner says of him: 'One of the greatest, most gigantic spirits of the British realm stands quite close to the opposition against what is merely commercial within the British commercial empire,

and that is James I. James I brings in a new element by continuously inoculating into the substance of the British people something that they will have forever, something that they must not lose if they are not to fall utterly into materialism. What it is that he inoculates into them is something that is linked by underground channels to the whole of the rest of European culture. Here we are confronted by a significant mystery.' (Lecture of 15 January 1917, *Karma of Untruthfulness*, Vol. II.) Steiner did not say explicitly what this 'inoculation' was, but he clearly regarded James as an extremely significant individuality for Britain. And especially in view of later events, such as the Civil War, James's reign was indeed a crucial time, not least in terms of the relationship between Freemasonry and Rosicrucianism.

24. For an illuminating discussion of the differences between the ahrimanic force of seduction, which seeks to enslave the ego, and the asuric force of destruction, which would annihilate it altogether, see A. Reuveni, *In the Name of the New World Order*, Temple Lodge Publishing 1996, pp.118–32.

Notes to Chapter 2 (pages 50–83)

1. *The Karma of Untruthfulness*, Vol. 1, RSP 1988, p.7.
2. Fischer Taschenbuch Verlag, Frankfurt 1983, pp.28–30.
3. Verlag Die Kommenden, Freiburg im Breisgau.
4. See Chapter 1 of this book, pp.35–36.
5. *Guardian Weekly*, 8 March 1992.
6. '... international life will be seen increasingly as a competition not between rival ideologies — since most economically successful states will be organized along similar lines — but between different cultures.' Francis Fukuyama, *The End of History and The Last Man*, The Free Press, New York 1992, p.234.
7. Re. the incarnation of Ahriman see pp.13–14. There is also another potential threat to Americanism, which lies dormant at present, namely, that of a recrudescent East Asian spirituality allied with political and economic forces, such as was seen in Japan from 1868 to 1945; China is an unknown

quantity in this respect, and Japan itself is examining its own future direction. In his highly significant book (see Note 6), Francis Fukuyama, Japanese-American former deputy director of the State Department's Policy Planning Staff, argues that fundamentalist Islam and an East Asian paternalistic authoritarianism constitute the 'new authoritarian alternatives, perhaps never before seen in history [which] may assert themselves in the future' (p.235). 'The most significant challenge being posed to the liberal universalism of the American and French revolutions today ... [is from] those societies in Asia which combine liberal economies with a kind of paternalistic authoritarianism' (p.238).

8. *The Wise Men – Six Friends and the World They Made,* Walter Isaacson and Evan Thomas, Faber & Faber 1986. Kennan, a diplomat, worked at the US Embassy in Moscow in the 1930s and 1940s and, after his return to the US in 1947, in State Department Policy Planning.

9. 'Marking his most explicit and highest-profile foreign policy role since resigning the presidency in 1974 ... Nixon told the conference ... [that] Russia may turn to "a new despotism" which could be "a far more dangerous threat to peace and freedom, and particularly to peace, than was the old Soviet totalitarianism".' (Reported in *The Washington Post* and quoted in *Guardian Weekly,* 22 March 1992.)

10. See Fukuyama, op. cit., note 6.

11. In a lecture of 21 February 1920, Steiner said the following about secrecy in English-speaking societies: '... they meet in the ceremonial of empty words, which in turn joins them together on the basis of a real spiritual foundation ... It is rather remarkable that in the age of empty words that hold sway in public life there should appear a spiritual community with decidedly effective principles! This spiritual community is very secretive, not so much as regards its membership but with regard to its actual internal intentions. Why is this happening? It is happening because empty words make it possible to falsify realities.' (*Ideas for a New Europe,* RSP 1992, p.65.) Every spiritual initiate who seeks to work in the exoteric field, i.e. within social life, requires assistants, a fellowship, a 'brotherhood', to help him carry out his work. The

principle of the secret Freemasonic lodge has been continued by powerful groups of businessmen, politicians, academics, media bosses and military men, etc., at whose regular meetings the world's media are forbidden attendance. Such groups include the Bilderberg Group (founded 1954 by Prince Bernhard of the Netherlands and the shadowy Josef Retinger) and the Trilateral Commission (founded 1972–73 by David Rockefeller and Zbigniew Brzezinski). The first was founded to maintain élite connections between America and Europe, the second to extend these to Japan. A powerful such group in Britain is the Royal Institute of International Affairs (Chatham House) founded 1919 by men who were either members of or were closely connected with Lord Milner's 'kindergarten' of advisers. The RIIA annual report of 1992–93 mentions the Chatham House Rule: 'When a meeting, or part thereof, is held under the Chatham House Rule, participants are free to use the information received, but neither the identity nor the affiliation of the speaker(s), nor that of any other participant, may be revealed; nor may it be mentioned that the information was received at a meeting of the Institute.'

12. For a discussion of the influence of French occult groups at the Russian Court after the 1890s, see S.O. Prokofieff's two books *The Spiritual Origins of Eastern Europe and the Future Mysteries of the Holy Grail*, Temple Lodge 1993, pp208–13, and *The Case of Valentin Tomberg*, Temple Lodge 1997, pp.41–48.

13. *Guardian Weekly*, 8 March 1992.

14. For a discussion of Vatican plans to resurrect the Holy Roman Empire and the role of a Franco-German-Polish axis in this, see A. Reuveni, *In the Name of the New World Order*, Temple Lodge 1996, p.103ff.

15. *Le Monde*, quoted in *Guardian Weekly*, 15 March 1992.

16. Carrington was joint president of the RIIA in 1995, a former director-general of NATO 1984–88, a member of the Trilateral Commission and chairman of the Bilderberg Group from 1991. He is an intimate friend of Henry Kissinger (and a founder member of Kissinger Associates), Lionel Rothschild and Conrad Black, Canadian owner of the Hollinger media empire. He was the Foreign Secretary in the lead-up to the

Falklands War in 1982, who oversaw the end of Rhodesian independence in 1979 (the new country Zimbabwe is effectively controlled by western mining interests). He was also the first EU envoy to be sent to deal with the Bosnia crisis in 1992. After his 'failure' he was replaced by David Owen, also a Bilderberger and Trilateral Commission member.

17. *The Karma of Untruthfulness*, Vol. 1, RSP 1988, p.40.
18. For all these Kissinger quotes, see Note 5 above.
19. *Guardian Weekly*, 22 March 1992. Drafted under the supervision of Paul Wolfowitz, undersecretary for policy, the memo was 'not supplied to Congress and not intended for public release'.
20. For Monnet, see *Jean Monnet — Memoirs*, Collins 1978, and François Duchene, *Jean Monnet — The First Statesman of Interdependence*, W.W. Norton & Co., New York 1994. Intimately connected with the highest echelons of Anglo-American power-brokers from his twenties during the First World War when he worked in London coordinating the economic side of the Anglo-French war effort, Jean Monnet (1888–1979) went on to do similar work in Washington — where he was personally sent by Churchill — during the Second World War. He was the real architect of the European Coal and Steel Community (1950), which was the precursor of the European Economic Community (1957). He also promoted Euratom and worked indefatigably as leader of the Action Committee for the United States of Europe (ACUSE), remaining in close touch with his powerful friends in Washington. After his first meeting with President Kennedy, Monnet wrote to Konrad Adenauer: 'The men around (JFK) have been well chosen. Our friends McCloy and Acheson have very important roles and enjoy great influence ... It is urgently necessary to organize the West — continental Europe, Great Britain, the USA, Canada ... the central core of this organization is the EC, at the heart of which is unity between Germany and France ... Equality is only possible now because France and Germany together have begun to build a great European entity with the prospect of becoming a sort of second America.' (*Monnet — Memoirs*.) Of this goal Kennedy said: 'Ever since the war, the reconstruction and knitting together

of Europe have been objectives of US policy, for we have recognized with you that in unity lies strength.' To Jean Monnet, JFK said: 'Under your inspiration Europe has come closer to unity in less than 20 years than it had done before in a thousand.' (Ibid.) In 1966 Monnet wrote down his credo in nine points, which included the following: 7. 'We must organize the collective action of our civilization. How can that be done? Only by uniting in collective action Europe and America which together have the greatest resources in the world, which share the same civilization, and which conduct their public affairs in the same democratic manner. 8. This organization, while seeking a state of coexistence with the East, will create a new world order and at the same time make possible the necessary and unconditional aid and support that our civilization, which must be preserved, will bring to the rest of the world.' (Ibid.) At the EC Commission Monnet Centenary gathering in Brussels on 10 November 1988, Jacques Delors said: 'The topics we are discussing here today are only of interest to a select few. There has been a poll which shows that only 7% of Europeans have ever heard of Jean Monnet.' Such was the secret effectiveness with which Monnet worked. Pascal Fontaine, Professor at the Paris Institute of Political Studies, said at the same gathering: 'How did ACUSE operate? Like an iceberg — only the tip was made public.' François Duchêne, Monnet's biographer and co-worker in ACUSE, said at the meeting in honour of his mentor: 'Jean Monnet laid the foundation of European orthodoxy which still underlies, though sometimes at a considerable depth, the theory and practice of the Community. More than a doctrine, it meant instilling habits of behaviour.' Those habits of Monnet's were habits of maximum secretiveness, in which the decisions of a few members of the Euro-élite could determine the destinies of millions.

Polish-born Joseph Retinger (1888–1960) was an even more shadowy figure than Monnet. He played a major role behind the scenes for European unity after the Second World War and was primarily responsible, with Prince Bernhard of the Netherlands, for bringing about the creation of the Bilderberg Group in May 1954, a clandestine congress of Euro-American élite members that has met regularly ever since and helps to coordinate the policy of the Anglo-American élites with those of continental countries. See John Pomian, *Joseph Retinger, Memoirs of an Éminence Grise*, Sussex University Press 1972.

21. There is no single detailed English language study of the Council of 869; see Heinz Herbert Schoeffler (ed.), *Der Kampf um das Menschenbild*, Verlag am Goetheanum 1986. A short English account is given in A.P. Shepherd, *The Battle for the Spirit – The Church and Rudolf Steiner*, Anastasi, Broome 1994, pp.67–83.

Notes to Chapter 3 (pages 84–155)

1. Huntington was a member of the CFR's 14-man Coordinating Group which oversaw the CFR 1980s Project, first mentioned in the CFR annual report of 1974. This was a long-range project that aimed to 'come to grips with strategies for modifying the behaviour of all the relevant actors in the international community – individuals, governments, agencies within governments, élite groups, industrial firms, interest groups, mass societies, and other groups and organizations at the subnational and trans-national levels' (from a CFR memorandum quoted in Shoup & Mintner, p.256). The bulk of the funds for the project came from the Ford, Lilly, Mellon, and Rockefeller Foundations. The 1980s Project sought to create a New World Order for the 1980s and beyond. By 1990, it had clearly succeeded; Soviet Communism was effectively down and out, and the New World Order itself was publicly declared by key CFR member President George Bush.

2. '...the rules, goals, and procedures that the advanced countries adopt to govern economic relationships with one another should be the norms of the global system. In other words, the arrangements among the advanced countries would be the central core of the wider system; other countries would be expected in time to join the central core.' (From the first publication of the 1980s project: 'The Management of Interdependence; A Preliminary View', quoted in Shoup & Mintner, pp.264–66.)

3. K. Wilson, ed. *British Foreign Secretaries and Foreign Policy: From Crimean War to First World War*, Croom Helm, London 1987.

4. Rifkind repeated his call for a transatlantic free trade area at the Conservative Party conference in Blackpool in October 1995, though again, the media did not highlight the proposal.

5. See Carroll Quigley, *The Anglo-American Establishment*, Chapter 3, and *Tragedy and Hope*, Macmillan, New York 1966, pp.949–55.

6. C.G. Harrison, *The Transcendental Universe — Six Lectures on Occult Science, Theosophy, and the Catholic Faith*, Temple Lodge, New York 1994, p.99. Very little is known about either Harrison or the Berean Society. Born in 1855, he regarded himself as a Christian esotericist, or 'theoretical occultist' of the Anglo-Catholic High Church persuasion, and the Berean Society was a society of people interested in similar things. See Christopher Bamford's comprehensive introduction to the above book for a discussion of the esoteric groups and ideas that formed the background and context to Harrison's lectures.

7. Harrison, p.98.

8. Lecture of 17 March 1916, GA 174b, *Die geistigen Hintergründe des Ersten Weltkrieges* (The Spiritual Origins of the First World War).

9. Penguin Books 1979.

10. The young assassin who sparked the First World War in Sarajevo in 1914 was named Gavrilo Princip — literally Prince, or Lord Gabriel; the man he murdered, Crown Prince Archduke Franz Ferdinand, was trying to transform the Austro-Hungarian Empire from an exclusive duopoly to a more cosmopolitan, all-inclusive triadic form.

11. I am preparing an extensive research on the subject. Suffice it to say that, in addition to the way the number is written into the very structure of the earth (its axial inclination is $23°$, which creates the effect of the seasons and consequent cultural manifestations) and into the human organism (the lungs, for instance, are based on the ratio of 2:3), from an anthroposophical point of view, it is significant that $869 - 666 = 203$; that the ratio of $333:666:869 = 3:2$; that $869 \times 2.3 = 1998.7$, and that 666×3 also $= 1998$. Indeed, if we are awake, we shall

notice this number all around us everywhere in daily life today; the media are constantly suggesting it to us. The year 1923 was, of course, that of the 'crucifixion' and 'resurrection' of the Anthroposophical Society during Rudolf Steiner's lifetime. Intimately related to the number 5, 23 is *the* number of man on earth; it is the number of choice for humanity, and today, as Rudolf Steiner so often warned, humanity is faced with the choice between higher development and the abyss of barbarism. Will we embrace dualistic thinking, which can only intensify the path into materialism, or threefoldness, which can regain for us the path to a wholesome view of the relationship between 'spirit' and 'matter'? Two or Three? This is the choice facing humanity today.

12. Both quotations from Christopher Hitchens, *Blood, Class, and Nostalgia – Anglo-American Ironies*, Chatto & Windus, London 1990, p.309.

13. See Glenn Davis and John G. Roberts, *An Occupation Without Troops – Wall Street's Half-Century Domination of Japanese Politics*, Yenbooks, Tokyo 1996, for the ways in which Japan has functioned as an American military and economic colony since 1945.

14. Freemasonry has traditionally been divided into two categories: 'operative', by which is meant associations or lodges of working stonemasons, which were found all over Europe in the Middle Ages; and 'speculative', which was a British phenomenon that emerged in the early seventeenth century and concerned itself only with the symbolic and occult aspects of architecture and geometry. It thus divorced itself from the real manual craft element of the path of knowledge that had existed in medieval times. Speculative Freemasonry quickly became dominated by members of the British squirearchy, aristocracy and royalty. And after the foundation of the Grand Lodge in London in 1717 and the formulation of the Constitutions of speculative Freemasonry in 1723 (Freemasonic Year 5723), its overseas networks were put to the service of British imperial policy. See D. Stevenson, *The Origins of Freemasonry – Scotland's Century 1590–1710*, Cambridge University Press 1988, J. Hamill, *The Craft – A History of English Freemasonry*, Crucible 1986, and R. Hyam,

Britain's Imperial Century 1815–1914 – A Study of Empire and Expansion, B.T. Batsford, London 1976, pp.152–56.

15. For the threefold occult nature of Asia, Europe and America, see R. Steiner, *The Tension Between East and West* (GA 83), Anthroposophic Press 1983, p.148ff., and also R. Steiner, *The Challenge of the Times* (GA 186), Anthroposophic Press 1941, pp.70–119.

16. For the 'metabolic' instinctive nature of thinking in the English-speaking peoples, see R. Steiner, *The Karma of Untruthfulness*, Vol. 2 (GA 174), Rudolf Steiner Press 1992, pp.91–139, and *The Challenge of the Times* (see Note 10 above), pp.202–14. The English-speaking peoples are above all concerned with the lower nature of man, the region of the will, in the limbs, the metabolic system, and the sexual organs. Here they find reality in the forces of destruction and transformation which take place there. It is the realm of the Father in the human organism, not the Son or the Holy Spirit. But the forces of breakdown and annihilation that exist there they allow to rise up into their thinking and this leads to the fascination with death, violence, murder, crime and lust, which especially pervades American culture and is spread via Hollywood throughout the world. The English-speaking peoples will find their true way only when they turn from the destructive but necessary forces that live in the metabolism to the other metabolic forces of transformation and renewal.

17. See S.O. Prokofieff, *The Spiritual Origins of Eastern Europe and the Future Mysteries of The Holy Grail*, Temple Lodge 1993, pp.315–50. Rudolf Steiner indicated that since the year 1802 western Freemasonry and the Jesuit Order have been tacitly cooperating with and infiltrating each other: 'From then onwards [from around 1802] the spheres of responsibility are clearly differentiated, but their sights are set all the more effectively upon an unequivocal world-rulership. The ideological and spiritual concerns are given exclusively into the hands of the Jesuits; the economic into those of the Anglo-American lodges, the lodges of the West.' (Quoted in S.O. Prokofieff, ibid. p.320.) Examples of this process of reciprocal action have been: the prevention of Kaspar Hauser's mission in Central Europe (see S.O. Prokofieff op. cit., p.321ff; the

machinations behind the diplomatic revolution of 1894–1907 which led to the First World War (see R. Riemeck, *Mitteleuropa – Bilanz eines Jahrhunderts*, Fischer Taschenbuch Verlag, Frankfurt 1983, pp.17–33); the parallelism of Vatican II under John XXIII and the Presidency of the first Catholic US President J.F. Kennedy; the P2 lodge scandal in Italy; the 'Holy Alliance' between John Paul II and Ronald Reagan to destabilize Communist Poland and hasten the end of Communism 1982–89 (see *Time* magazine, 24 February 1992); and Zbigniew Brzezinski's plans for a Franco-Polish-German axis in Europe (see Reuveni, op. cit. pp.77–104).

18. In a *TE* article entitled 'The International Order' exactly a year after the article under consideration here, the following words appear: 'If at the moment some of these [Islamic] revivalists are fiercely anti-western, before long they will probably discover that they face even worse arguments with Russia about the disputed borderlands of Central Asia...' (*TE*, 24 December 1994 – 6 January 1995, p.18).

19. For the significance of Poland to Washington and the Vatican, see A. Reuveni, *In the Name of the 'New World Order' – Manifestations of Decadent Powers in World Politics*, Temple Lodge 1996, pp.78–117.

20. For a fascinating study of this process, see C. Hitchens, *Blood, Class and Nostalgia – Anglo-American Ironies*, Chatto & Windus, London 1990.

21. See R. Hyam, op. cit. p.170. In the early nineteenth century the British Foreign Minister George Canning wrote about his 'apprehension of the ambition and ascendency of the United States of America [whose purpose was to organize] a transatlantic league of which it would have the sole direction.' Hyam, p.168, also quotes R.W. van Alstyne, *The American Empire* (Hist. Assoc. pamphlet 1960), p.15: '...as van Alstyne writes, what really counted was "the hidden positives to the effect that the United States shall be the only colonizing power in North America and that it shall be the directing power in both North and South America. This is imperialism preached in the grand manner, for the only restrictions placed upon the directing power are those which it imposes upon itself. The Monroe Doctrine would be better described as the

Monroe manifesto".' Hyam also notes that 'the American empire pursued a global pattern of expansion from the very beginning of the century. Alexander Hamilton in 1787 talked of the United States 'becoming "the arbiter of Europe in America". Soon she was thrusting politically in all directions — only the thrust towards Canada was halted; and that not until the present century. As late as 1911 the American mind was reluctant to admit defeat in this direction.'

22. Conflict between Freemasonry and the Jesuits reached a climax in 1773, 35 years after Freemasons were declared excommunicate by the Papacy in 1738. Freemasons infiltrated Catholic countries to such an extent that in 1773 they succeeded in getting Pope Clement XIV to suppress the Jesuit Order. The Jesuits went underground, and found succour especially in Russia under Catherine II where their services as educators were valued. Here their pupil Joseph de Maistre (1754–1821), French-born Sardinian ambassador at St Petersburg, was especially active in spreading Jesuitical ideas and combating the influence of Central European Rosicrucianism in Russia (see S.O. Prokofieff, *The Spiritual Origins*... pp.201–05, and 295–97). On the defensive after their proscription by the Vatican, the Jesuits apparently decided that a compromise of sorts would have to be made with Freemasonry, which led to the arrangement of 1802 mentioned in Note 12 above. Rudolf Steiner noted that 'at a particular point in time, from the end of the eighteenth century, the Masonic Orders swarmed with Jesuits, and in certain orders they made the highest grades' (lecture of 3 July 1920, GA 198, *Heilfaktoren für den sozialen Organismus*). Freemasonry in Britain experienced its own division during the period 1751–1813. In 1813 the split between the two main Masonic factions (the Antients [sic] and the Moderns) was healed, and the following year Pope Pius VII restored both the Jesuit Order and the Inquisition. Caspar Hauser had been born in 1812. The P2 lodge scandal in Italy, which came to light in the early 1980s, gave further evidence of the degree to which, still today, the Vatican is infiltrated by Freemasons.

23. Published by The Free Press (Macmillan Inc.), New York 1992.

24. This comes from the second of the seven wills drawn up by Cecil Rhodes, written on 2 June 1877, the day he became a Freemason. See *The Randlords*, pp.140–41. Rhodes consciously based his secret society on Freemasonic and Jesuit models. It is noteworthy that his first will, written in 1872, before he became a Freemason, merely left all his wealth to the British Colonial Secretary 'to be used at his discretion for the expansion of the British Empire'. For further evidence of the evolution of Rhodes' plans, including their metamorphosis as the USA took the imperial baton from Britain, see Carroll Quigley, *The Anglo-American Establishment*, and *Tragedy and Hope*, p.950ff; and Christopher Hitchens, *Blood, Class, and Nostalgia* (especially Chapter 9). No sensationalist or militia apologist is Quigley, but rather one who worked within the bowels of the American East Coast academic and foreign policy establishment and even, in his own words, shared many of its goals. He claims to have been given access to the papers of the group (he calls it the Milner Group, after Alfred, Lord Milner, Rhodes' key lieutenant and successor). He then 'blew the whistle' on their plans in his two books (mentioned above) because he felt that the group should be less secretive about its aims. The result was that *The Anglo-American Establishment* (1949) could not find a publisher until 1981 and *Tragedy and Hope* (1966) was soon withdrawn from publication by Macmillan. Quigley had to fight for years to get the publishers' plates returned to him. A professor at Georgetown University, the Jesuit-founded college that has provided so many American diplomats with an education in foreign affairs, Quigley was also Bill Clinton's teacher and was specifically mentioned by him in his 1992 Democratic Party nomination acceptance speech. See Introduction to this book, p.18.

25. Peter Collier and David Horowitz, *The Rockefellers – An American Dynasty*, Jonathan Cape, London 1976, p.319 *et passim*. In *Foreign Affairs* (April 1974), the CFR journal, Richard N. Gardner, former deputy assistant secretary of state for international organizations under Presidents Kennedy and Johnson, wrote: '... the house of world order will have to be built from the bottom up rather than from the top

down... An end run around national sovereignty, eroding it piece by piece, will accomplish much more than the old-fashioned assault.' Brook Chisholm, director of the UN World Health Organization (WHO) stated that: 'To achieve world government, it is necessary to remove from the minds of men their individualizm, loyalty to family traditions, national patriotism and religious dogmas.' (Gardner and Chisholm quoted in Pat Robertson, *The New World Order*, Word Publishing, Dallas, 1991, pp.6–7.) One can see how such sentiments could easily appeal to liberal minds.

26. Hitchens, *Blood, Class, and Nostalgia*, p.251.
27. Rudolf Steiner, lecture of 15 January 1917 (GA 174), *The Karma of Untruthfulness*, Vol. 2, RSP 1992.
28. In *TE* 24 December 1994–6 January 1995 (pp.17–18), this idea was still being pushed: 'The 21st century's probable contenders for power (Russia; China; Europe and America either separately *or together* [emphasis TMB]; and some new Muslim entity)...' Later in the same article, we read: '...nobody is now in a position to invade or atomize either Europe or America. That will remain true until and unless a hostile China becomes a global power, Russia returns to enmity with the West, or somebody organizes an expansionary Islamic power out of the present chaos between Iran and Morocco; and, though one or more of those things is almost certain to happen eventually, it is unlikely to happen in the next few years...'
29. The third of the article's three illustrations (see p.132) shows a canny insight into East Asian cultural images: a fearsome dragon's head is shown rising out of clouds like a nuclear explosion above the sea by which are seen two figures with the Japanese flag between them bowing in submission. In Japan and China dragons are traditionally elemental creatures associated with clouds and sea, hence the demonstration explosion off the Japanese coast. Ever since the early days of communication between Chinese and Japanese emperors when one of the former wrote addressing the ruler of Japan as his servant, and the latter replied, 'Hail to the ruler of the land of the setting sun from the ruler of the land of the rising sun!' Japan has been fiercely independent of China. Although there

are today not a few Japanese who argue that Japan should throw in its lot with China, no self-respecting Japanese would look at this illustration without feeling a measure of indignation.

30. Rudolf Steiner indicated that the Mongoloid peoples of North-east Asia were under the leadership of Mars beings, spiritual beings who are active from the spiritual sphere of Mars, and that there is a spiritual centre in the North China plain in which the Mars Oracle—the receptacle of the impulses of such beings—located itself after leaving Atlantis. See R. Steiner, *The Mission of Folk Souls in Connection with Germanic-Scandinavian Mythology*, Spiritual Research Editions, New York 1989, pp.75–76. Modern anthropology would not recognize that the Chinese and the Mongolians belonged to the same race and would insist on a narrower definition of each group; nevertheless, common sense tells us that the peoples of North-east Asia (Han Chinese and other Chinese, Japanese, Koreans, Manchus, Tibetans and Mongols as well as the less numerous Tartar or Turkic peoples) do indeed all belong to the same race and share similar physical and even psychological and cultural characteristics just as do, say, Basques, Anglo-Saxons, Romanians and Russians. (In the same lecture cycle Steiner speaks of Europeans, the Caucasian people, as being under the influence of Jupiter spirits and the Jupiter Oracle as having been located in northern Germany.)

31. Lecture of 17 September 1916 (GA 171), *Inner Impulses of Evolution*, AP 1984.

32. See, for example, *The East in the Light of the West* (Note 10 above), and also C.G. Harrison, *The Transcendental Universe*, Lecture 2, Temple Lodge 1993.

33. See Note 19 above.

34. The oil industry really got underway after the beginning of the Age of Michael (1879), but oil is actually a form of energy that arose out of the impulses of the Age of Gabriel (1525–1879). There is no contradiction here. The colossal spiritual forces of the archangelic Time Regents do not stop on a sixpence! They are at their peak at the end of their period of 'office' and continue to be very strong during the first century

of the succeeding archangelic era, while the impulse of the
next Time Regent is gradually fading in. As the Age of
Michael has progressed, more and more attention has
focused on non-subterranean, non-fossil-fuel energies (wind,
wave, solar power, etc.) which are more related to the sun and
the living elements rather than the mineral earth. Oil and gas
thus become increasingly 'illegitimate' out-of-time forms of
energy in the Age of Michael and work destructively in the
service of evil. The harmful geopolitical consequences of oil
exploration are an example of this.

35. See Derek Wilson, *Rothschild – A Story of Wealth and Power*,
    Andre Deutsch, London 1988.
36. *Foreign Affairs*, Vol. 72, No. 3, pp.42–45.
37. See Note 25.
38. Ibid., p.44.
39. Ibid., pp.44–45.
40. Ibid., p.45.
41. Ibid., p.47.
42. Reports in *The Economist* (15 November 1997, p.86) and *The
    World In 1998* (*Economist* Publications, p.117) indicate that the
    Chinese may not have reckoned with the Muslim Uighur
    guerillas of their westernmost province, Xinjiang, through
    which the Chinese government wishes to lay a gigantic oil
    pipeline from the Caspian Sea area of Kazakhstan to China
    proper, thus providing for most of China's burgeoning oil
    needs. Reduced to only 54 per cent of the population of the
    land they call East Turkestan because of the nearly 6m Han
    Chinese whom Beijing have in recent years settled in
    Xinjiang, and bitter about their declining employment
    prospects and the Chinese pressure on their culture and
    religion, the Uighurs have taken to armed uprisings; the
    Chinese have responded with their customary severity. This
    problem will get worse, and world attention on Tibet will
    only exacerbate it. A vicious spiral is likely to set in, because
    the Chinese know that if they allow more autonomy for Tibet
    the Uighurs will press for the same. No vital oil pipeline is
    going to pass through Tibet, however. Beijing, which has
    ruled East Turkestan/Xinjiang intermittently since 1759, will
    not allow a Uighur autonomy to control what may well

become the jugular vein of China's economy. China's involvement in this new version of the nineteenth-century Anglo-Russian 'Great Game' in Central Asia may well lead to conflict with Russia or the new Muslim states of Central Asia. Washington has seemed phlegmatic about China's participation in the 'game'. Perhaps that may have something to do with the fact that America's favourite state in the region is Uzbekistan, where since the collapse of Soviet Communist control calls for a new Muslim superstate—Turkestan—which would embrace the whole of Central Asia have been most vocal. This situation is an example of the dire geopolitical consequences of the struggle for the control of oil supplies and the territory in which they lie.

43. Alexandre Kojève (1902–68) gave a series of very influential seminars at the École Pratique des Hautes Études in Paris in the 1930s. He misinterpreted Hegel via both Marx and Heidegger and his ideas had a tremendous influence on the next generation of French radical thinkers, leftist postmodernists such as Raymond Queneau, Georges Bataille and Michel Foucault, as well as American postmodernists on the right (Leo Strauss, Allan Bloom and Francis Fukuyama). An ironic admirer of Stalin, Kojève worked in his later life as a bureaucrat for the European Economic Community.

44. Fukuyama, p.330.

45. Ibid., p.334–35.

46. Ibid., p.336.

47. Ibid., pp.337–38.

48. Ibid., p.338.

49. Ibid., p.338.

50. Ibid., p.339.

51. Ibid., p.338.

52. Ibid., pp.338–39.

53. Ibid., p.339.

54. Eighteenth-century French intellectuals and political thinkers of the pre-revolutionary era, notably Voltaire, Rousseau and the Encyclopaedists, were profoundly influenced by John Locke (1632–1704) and David Hume (1711–76), the two leading British empiricist thinkers. While they perhaps cannot, strictly speaking, be called materialistic philosophers, the

thought of the empiricists recognized the primacy of sense data which the mind merely reflected upon, and thus laid the basis for the more thoroughgoing materialist philosophies of the nineteenth-century. The radical sceptic Hume sought to show that causality was a myth: '...there could be no necessary connection between distinct events. All that remains ... is a series of fleeting perceptions with no external object, no enduring subject to whom they could belong, and not themselves even bound to one another.' Hume famously wrote: 'Reason is, and ought only to be the slave of the passions, and can never pretend to any other office than to serve and obey them.' Dunn, Urmson and Ayer, *The British Empiricists*, OUP, 1992, pp.194–95, 200, 202.

55. Huntington, p.49.
56. Fukuyama, pp.310–11.
57. Ibid., pp.311–312. *TE* double issue, December 23 1995 – January 5 1996 included an article on the future of the nation state: 'The Shape of the World – The nation state is dead. Long live the nation state'. Its closing sentences were as follows: 'Like the natural world, the world of geopolitics does not easily change its species. The coming century will still be the home of recognizable beasts: muscular lions and fearful deer, lumbering rhinos and cunning jackals. That may be a pity, but the inhabitants of the jungle have to live with it.'
58. Fukuyama, op. cit., pp.308–09.
59. Quoted in Fukuyama, op. cit., pp.308–09.